H. H. Price was Wykeham Professor of Logic in the University of Oxford from 1935 to 1959. His publications include *Perception*, *Hume's Theory of the External World* (Clarendon Press, 1940), *Belief*, and *Thinking and Experience*. He was President of the Society for Psychical Research in 1939–40 and 1960–1.

ESSAYS IN
THE PHILOSOPHY OF
RELIGION

ESSAYS IN
THE PHILOSOPHY OF
RELIGION

———

H. H. PRICE

Based on
THE SARUM LECTURES
1971

OXFORD
AT THE CLARENDON PRESS
1972

Oxford University Press, Ely House, London W. 1

GLASGOW NEW YORK TORONTO MELBOURNE WELLINGTON
CAPE TOWN IBADAN NAIROBI DAR ES SALAAM LUSAKA ADDIS ABABA
DELHI BOMBAY CALCUTTA MADRAS KARACHI LAHORE DACCA
KUALA LUMPUR SINGAPORE HONG KONG TOKYO

PRINTED IN GREAT BRITAIN
AT THE UNIVERSITY PRESS, OXFORD
BY VIVIAN RIDLER
PRINTER TO THE UNIVERSITY

PREFACE

THESE essays are a revised version of the Sarum Lectures delivered in Oxford in 1971, and I should like to thank the University of Oxford most warmly for inviting me to deliver them.

For almost as long as I can remember I have been interested in two subjects, the Philosophy of Religion on the one hand and Psychical Research on the other, and in the relations between them. No doubt it would be a great mistake to identify the paranormal with the spiritual. For example, a mystical experience is very different from a telepathic dream. Both are beyond the normal, but they are beyond it in quite different ways. Nevertheless, there is an overlap between these two types of enquiry, the investigation of religious experiences on the one hand, and the investigation of paranormal phenomena on the other. For instance, the 'good news' of the Christian gospel is concerned, among other things, with life after death; and life after death is a subject on which psychical researchers have something to say. Again, a psychical researcher does not use the word 'miracle'. But some of the phenomena which a religious person calls miracles do fall within the psychical researcher's field of interest and can be explained in terms of telepathy or clairvoyance or telekinesis.

In these lectures therefore I have tried to describe how a philosopher who is interested in psychical research might approach some of the problems of religion, and to consider what insight we can derive from this approach. Whether in doing so I have succeeded in providing that 'support of the Christian Faith' which the Statute requires of the Sarum Lecturer the reader must judge. I trust that at least I have put no stumbling-block in his way.

H. H. P.

Oxford
February 1972

CONTENTS

1

PRINCIPIUM SAPIENTIAE TIMOR DOMINI

RELIGIOUS experience is an embarrassing subject. We must try to speak of it 'from within'. How can we do justice to it otherwise? But then we find that the heart enters into it as well as the head. A religious person is not only one who accepts a certain sort of theoretical world-outlook. He also has —and not only has, but cultivates—certain sorts of emotional attitudes and even thinks that his theoretical world-outlook requires them. In theistic religion, and especially in Christian theism, the most important of these emotional attitudes are love on the one hand and fear on the other. 'God-fearing' is a term of commendation, or at any rate it used to be. We are even told in the Book of Proverbs (9: 10) that the fear of the Lord is the beginning of wisdom: 'Principium sapientiae timor Domini'.

No doubt the fear of the Lord might conceivably be the beginning of wisdom, but only the beginning. This, however, does not seem to be the Christian view. According to Christian teaching, this fear of the Lord is not only the beginning of wisdom, as the author of this passage in Proverbs says it is. It is not merely something we must have in the early stages of our earthly pilgrimage but can dispense with later. On the contrary, we have to retain it to the very end. For instance, in the prayer for the Church Militant we find the phrase 'all thy servants departed this life in thy faith and fear'. Elsewhere, in the Burial Service (last collect) we find an even more remarkable phrase 'that blessing which thy well-beloved Son shall then pronounce to all that love and fear thee'; and these are the persons who are to receive 'the kingdom prepared for them from the beginning of the world'. Can love and fear be combined? It seems that they can be, and they should be, even when the Christian's earthly pilgrimage has come to an end.

This combination of love and fear is at first sight highly paradoxical. The difficulty is that fear seems to be a *hostile* attitude. We fear what is harmful to us or what we believe to be so. Fear has many different sorts of objects. We may fear a living creature, whether man or beast. We may fear to do something, for instance to go out of doors in a thunderstorm or to jump into icy water. We may fear to refrain from doing something, for instance to refrain from shutting the front door in a visitor's face if he has a ferocious dog with him. We may fear to say something, for instance to 'own up' to something wrong or foolish we have done. We may fear to keep silence when some very angry and strong-willed person insists on being told some secret with which we have been entrusted. But all these different objects of fear have something in common. All of them are *evils*, or at least they seem to the fearing person to be so. To put it very simply, fear seems to be an 'anti-attitude'. We are 'against' something or someone that we fear. Love, on the contrary, is a 'pro-attitude'. Indeed it is *the* pro-attitude *par excellence*. We are 'for' something or some-one that we love.

But though we fear what is harmful to us, or at least what we believe to be harmful to us, it does not follow that fear itself is harmful to us. On the contrary, it is very often useful. The biological utility of fear is that it enables a living creature to escape death or injury. There are various ways of doing so. One is to run away. Another is to conceal oneself, as Adam and Eve tried to do in the Genesis story of the Fall. Sometimes the best way of doing this is to 'freeze', to remain absolutely motionless, because that makes it difficult for our enemy to perceive us. That is also the reason why camouflage, natural or artificial, is so useful. Many living creatures are protected from their enemies in this way, by what is called 'protective colouring'. But unfortunately for them, their enemies are often camouflaged too. The striped tiger is not easily detected among the shadows in the undergrowth; his domestic relative, the tabby cat, is not easily detected either. All this applies to human enemies also, though their camouflage has to be voluntarily devised and voluntarily assumed. Indeed, according to St. Paul, the same applies to the enemy of all mankind, Satan himself 'assumes the appearance of an angel of light' (μετασχηματίζεται εἰς ἄγγελον φωτός).¹

It is important to notice that there is something *cognitive* about fear. It makes sense to ask 'Whom or what do you fear?' Yet there is a curious difference here in the English language at any rate between 'fearing' and 'being (or feeling) afraid'. You can tell me what it is, or who it is, that you fear, or what it is that you fear to do. And usually you can answer if I ask you who it is that you are afraid of. Usually, but not always. Sometimes the answer is, 'I cannot tell you. I just feel afraid.' We can say, if we like, that what you are afraid of is 'the whole situation'; but still you cannot pick out any particular fear-inspiring feature of it. The same applies sometimes when the object of our fear is a person. 'What is there about him that frightens you?' Sometimes we cannot answer this question; or if we must make some answer, we can only say 'everything'. There may be places, as well as persons, which inspire this kind of indiscriminating fear: a certain room in a house, for instance, or the north-west corner of a certain wood. The kind of fear I speak of need not necessarily be intense, though sometimes it is. The interesting thing about it is that we cannot say just what it is that we are afraid of.

It is also important to notice that there are two other cognitive epithets which apply to fear. There are mistaken fears, and there are unreasonable fears. In both cases we are inclined to say 'there is really nothing to be afraid of'. But

---

¹ 2 Corinthians 11 : 14. I have assumed that the verb is in the middle voice. The A.V., however, takes it to be passive ('is transformed into'). In any case 'transform' is not the correct translation of the Greek verb μετασχηματίζειν, at any rate in modern English. Satan does not 'turn into' an angel of light. It is rather that he assumes the outward appearance or the visible qualities of an angel of light. (The same verb is used to describe the Transfiguration.)

there is an important difference between them. A mistaken fear need not necessarily be unreasonable. 'They were afraid where no fear was' may be an example of this.[1] Perhaps they did have quite good grounds for expecting to be attacked. And an unreasonable fear need not necessarily be mistaken. I had no reason to fear that I should arrive late at my meeting in London. I just happen to be a timorous person who always expects the worst. But this time, for once, my expectation was justified. The train I hoped to take never even started from Oxford, because the engine broke down at Birmingham.

Now—in connection with the *Fear* of the Lord—let us consider the rather terrifying words 'whom the Lord loveth he chastiseth and scourgeth every son that he receiveth'. We might think of this scourging and chastening not as a punishment, but as a test. If we ask to be received by him as sons, we are claiming that we love him. But do we love him for his own sake, or only because of the benefits we hope to receive from him? Do we want him even if he hurts us? The omniscient Lord knows what the answer to this question is. But perhaps we ourselves do not know until we have been chastened and scourged, and it is very important for us that we should know.

> Quemadmodum desiderat cervus ad fontes aquarum
> Ita desiderat anima mea ad te, Deus.
>
> Like as the hart desireth the water-brooks
> So longeth my soul after thee, O God.
>   (Psalm 42, Prayer Book version)

In all the Psalter, there are no words more moving than these. The hart desires the water-brooks so much that he does all he can to find them, even though the way to them is long and stony and there are thickets full of sharp thorns which he must struggle to get through. Is that true of us? Surely we must all wish that it may be. The Psalmist says that it is true of him.

But if the hart continues to seek the water-brooks, he may eventually find them. To use more traditional Christian

---

[1] Psalm 53: 5 (Prayer Book version).

terminology, he who is now *in via* ('on his way') may eventually find himself *in patria* ('in his own country'). We are told that our citizenship is in Heaven:

> Et ad Jerusalem e Babylonia
> Post longa regredi tandem exilia.[1]

If this hope is eventually fulfilled, will love still be combined with fear even then? Apparently it will, for the persons who are to receive the kingdom prepared for them from the beginning of the world are described as 'Those that love and fear thee'. It seems that in them at any rate there is no inconsistency between love and fear. Or rather, the author of this prayer did not think there was, nor did those who included it in the liturgy.

On the other hand, we are also told that 'perfect love casts out fear'.[2] The reason offered for this is 'because fear hath torment', κόλασιν ἔχει ('contains chastisement'). The verb κολάζειν means literally 'to curtail' or 'to dock', and hence 'to chastise'. The point seems to be that fear *diminishes* us somehow, 'makes us feel small' as we say. But perhaps there are more ways than one of being diminished; and perhaps there is more than one kind of fear too. The word 'awe' denotes a kind of fear which is by no means incompatible with love. Moreover, although we are 'diminished' by it, we are somehow exalted by it too, or even exalted *because* we are diminished. Let us remember too that the word *reverentia* originally denoted a kind of fear (from *vereor*, 'I fear'). It is unfortunate that in modern English the words 'awful' and 'reverent' have been so much devalued.

I venture to suggest that the fear which persists in the minds of the blessed in heaven is something like awestruck adoration; and though the 'belittlement' is still there, the sense of the Lord's infinite majesty, this is itself a cause of rejoicing. It is a kind of fusion of love and fear. They are His, but also He is theirs.

---

[1] Peter Abelard, '*O Quanta qualia*'.   [2] 1 John 4: 18.

THE CONCEPT OF 'THE SUBLIME'

Perhaps we can find something faintly analogous to this awestruck exaltation, this combination or fusion of fear and love, if we consider the aesthetic concept of 'the sublime'. There is a familiar distinction (first pointed out, I think, by Burke) between the beautiful and the sublime. For instance, it would be inadequate to describe Michelangelo's statue of Moses as 'beautiful' (still less could we call it 'pretty'). It is awe-inspiring, and we do feel diminished when we look at it; and yet we find a certain fulfilment or exaltation in being thus diminished.

The same is true of some spectacles in nature. There is a view of Mont Blanc which one may see from a hill about 5,000 feet high above St. Gervais in Haute-Savoie, looking across a valley a mile or two wide. I am thinking of this view now: the terrifying summit of the great mountain, glittering with ice; its crags and its pinnacles, most formidable, most menacing; and sometimes one may faintly hear the sound of an avalanche. And yet this spectacle, terrifying though it is, and even because it is terrifying, has a splendour, a magnificence, which no words of mine can describe. The spectator is at once diminished and exalted by it; and the fear, the littleness and powerlessness which he feels, is a necessary condition for the exaltation.

Again, anyone who has ever piloted a small aircraft and knows what it is like to fly through or near a cumulo-nimbus cloud (a thunder cloud) will probably have similar feelings whenever he contemplates such a cloud. He rejoices in it just because he knows from experience what a formidable thing it is. To me at any rate, a well-formed cumulo-nimbus cloud is one of the most splendid and fascinating spectacles in nature. I cannot resist mentioning another meteorological example. Emerson tells us somewhere about a negro cabin-boy who delighted in storms at sea. When there was a gale, he would say, 'Blow, me do tell you, blow!' The worse the weather was, the more he rejoiced in it.

FEAR CAN BE DESIRABLE

If we are still inclined to think that fear is something wholly undesirable, let us consider what we should lose if we were wholly fearless. It was said of Lord Nelson that he did not know what it is like to feel fear. This is not easy to believe. But if it was literally true, I think we should have to admire him less than we do. Can there be courage or self-sacrifice where there is no fear at all? Moreover, I think we should have to pity him. A totally fearless person would be missing something, something which we all value highly. There could be no thrills for such a person. Nothing would be for him an exciting adventure. How much fear a person can stand is no doubt a question of temperament. There is indeed a threshold above which fear becomes catastrophic; and the height of this threshold varies greatly from one person to another and even in the same person at different times. (Napoleon commended 'the courage of three o'clock in the morning' because that is the time when a person's vitality is at its lowest.) But how insipid our lives would be if we never at any time had any fear of anything! Nothing venture, nothing win. And how can you venture if you have no fear at all of losing? It has been said, I think, that the normal man is a betting animal. Taking risks is something he enjoys for its own sake.

FEAR 'ON BEHALF OF ...'

There is another kind of fear which is even more commendable; and this fear, so far from being incompatible with love, is actually a consequence of it. It has even been said that 'love is full of fears'—fears on behalf of someone whom one loves. The Blessed Virgin Mary may surely be regarded as the pattern of Christian love. Then what shall we say of the Flight into Egypt? Surely she was moved by fear on behalf of her Child? Again, 'Stabat Mater dolorosa Ante crucem lacrimosa'. Was there no fear there? I suggest, then, that the fear perfect love casts out is self-centred fear, fear on one's own behalf, but that it neither can nor should cast out fear on behalf of those whom one loves. I would also suggest that the 'tenderness' which is an element in at least some sorts of love is closely related to fear, fear on behalf of the person who is loved; there is something *protective* about it. And tenderness is surely something wholly admirable. If I may dare to say so, it is this tenderness which we see in the words *ante crucem lacrimosa.*

'SHEER FUNK'

But obviously there is nothing protective about the *timor Domini* which is the beginning of wisdom. Nor is there any tenderness in it. Each of us fears what is going to happen to *him* if he himself disobeys the Lord's commandments. It is not fear on another's behalf, but on one's own. Shall we say, then, that this fear of the Lord just consists in being frightened, frightened or terrified of the Lord's wrath or his judgements? According to this account of it, the *timor Domini* is what a schoolboy in my youth would have called 'sheer funk'. And indeed that may well have been what the headmaster hoped to produce in those bad old days, when he said of such a boy 'I am going to put the fear of God into him' and proceeded to give him six strokes of the birch. If this is the kind of fear referred to when it was said that the fear of the Lord is the beginning of wisdom, it is something very different indeed from the 'awestruck exaltation' which we have ventured to attribute to the Blessed in Heaven.

Moreover, if this is the kind of fear ('sheer funk') which the headmaster hoped to produce—just sheer terror of breaking the rules—would his success have been worth much? The boy would just have been taught to choose the lesser of two evils. He hates keeping the rules, but he hates bodily pain even more.

The application of this parable is fairly obvious. The moral philosophy of Proverbs is a 'reductionist' theory. According to this theory 'right' just means 'what God commands us to do', and 'wrong' just means 'what God forbids us to do'. But to make these rather paradoxical contentions more plausible, the writers of Proverbs also maintain that God commands us to do those actions (and only those) which tend to increase the long-term happiness of all his human creatures, and forbids us to do those actions (and only those) which tend to decrease the long-term happiness of all his human creatures. This theory might perhaps be described as 'theological utilitarianism'.

So far as I can see, the author or authors of Proverbs thought that the fear of the Lord was the beginning of both *sapientia* and *prudentia*, and indeed made no clear distinction between them. We even find one passage where *prudentia* is attributed to the Lord himself. 'Dominus sapientia fundavit terram, stabilivit caelos prudentia' (Proverbs 3: 19 where the Septuagint has ἡτοίμασεν δὲ οὐρανοὺς ἐν φρονήσει). It may be worth while to notice too that *prudentia* is a contracted form of *providentia*: and when we speak of the 'providence' of God, we do attribute to him something analogous to the prudence—the choice of appropriate means to an end—which we attribute to a practically-wise human being. This same reference to time, to the distinction between past, present, and future, is implicit in the Greek word φρόνησις, whereas σοφία, the equivalent of the Latin *sapientia*, is concerned not only with events in time, but also—or even primarily—with timeless truths. A great mathematician or logician would be *sapiens*, but he need not be *prudens*. When Syracuse was captured by the Romans, Archimedes was so intent on his geometrical studies that he failed to notice what was happening, and was killed by a Roman soldier.

It seems to me that when the authors of Proverbs are speaking of human beings (not of the Lord himself) the wisdom they refer to is always practical wisdom, even though in the Septuagint version of Proverbs they do often call it σοφία. If I am right, their doctrine is that the fear of the Lord is the beginning of *practical* wisdom, the wisdom which shows itself in conduct. Even so, I am not sure that they distinguished between doing what is right for its own sake, and doing what conduces to one's own long-term happiness. Perhaps if we could submit them to a viva voce examination, we should find that they were not very clear about the distinction between conscience on the one hand and rational self-love on the other, or (to use Kant's terminology instead of Butler's) between categorical and hypothetical imperatives.

A SCEPTICAL INTERPRETATION OF
PRINCIPIUM SAPIENTIAE TIMOR DOMINI

We may now notice a difficulty which did not occur to the authors of Proverbs, who lived in a wholly or almost wholly theistic society. There could be a sceptical interpretation of 'Principium sapientiae timor Domini'. An agnostic or even an atheist could agree that the fear of God is the beginning of practical or ethical wisdom, though he would emphasize the word 'beginning'. He would point out that a belief which is mistaken, or one which we have no reason for thinking correct, may have very important psychological and social effects. Indeed, it need not even be a belief. What Coleridge called 'a willing suspension of disbelief' may have such effects too.

Let us conceive of (1) a society in which the Bible is assiduously read by everyone, just as a work of imaginative literature, much as the plays of Shakespeare are or the novels of Dickens. No one even asks whether these biblical stories are true. But everyone reads them and ruminates on them and discusses them. Contrast this with (2) another society in which everyone believes the biblical narratives but no one takes any interest in them. No one is 'moved' by them or ruminates on them or discusses them with his neighbour. Their attitude is much like the one which most of us (regrettably) have to the history of Anglo-Saxon England. We believe what we read about King Ethelred the Unready, or even about Hengist and Horsa. But we seldom think about them or discuss them. These 'old, unhappy far-off things' do not affect our personal lives at all.

Which of these two societies is the more religious one? Obviously the first. Indeed, the second one is not religious at all; and though everyone in it assents to some of the statements which religious people make, their assent (to use Newman's terminology) is 'notional' rather than 'real'.

We can now see how there might be a sceptical interpretation of 'Principium sapientiae timor Domini', and how an agnostic or even an atheist might agree that the fear of the Lord is the beginning of wisdom. We can quite well conceive of a society in which all intelligent adults are agnostics or humanists. (We already live in one in which very many of them are.) And even there it might still be believed that the fear of God is the beginning of wisdom. These intelligent adults might very well agree that the belief in a righteous God who imposes sanctions on wrongdoing has great educative value. Here we have a very useful fairy-tale, an important instrument of moral education; and it will not have the desired effects if it is disbelieved by the young. Conceivably it need not be believed either. It may be enough if it never even occurs to the young to ask whether the fairy-tale is true. The mere thought of a righteous God who will punish you if you break any of the Ten Commandments may well suffice, if it is frequently attended to and always present at the back of your mind. That will be enough to keep you morally 'on the rails' for most of the time. Thereby you will acquire habits of right action and a tendency to feel very uncomfortable when you do wrong.

But when you are grown up, you are able to dispense with this thought of a righteous God. By that time, the fairy-tale has done its work, and you do not need it any more. Instead, you are ready to acquire the scientific outlook which is characteristic of a mature and intelligent human being. It is as if your legs were weak at first and you could only learn to walk straight by using a good big stick. But after a time you grow stronger and can walk straight for a few yards without it; and eventually you can dispense with the stick altogether.

To make this account of moral education more plausible, one might enlist the aid of the anthropologists. One might argue that in primitive societies, in the 'childhood' of the human race, the fear of supernatural beings of one sort or another had to continue throughout a person's life. At that time no one was grown up, except in a purely anatomical and physiological sense; and therefore the fear of God (or of the gods) was a necessary condition for maintaining that minimum of social cohesion and social co-operation without which no society can exist. Indeed, even in our own society there are some who never grow up, and they still need the help of the *timor Domini* throughout the whole of their lives. They never learn to walk straight without the aid of this stick, or at any rate they cannot do without it all the time. But if we gave as much attention to moral education as we now give to intellectual education, we might hope that the minority of 'weaker brethren' would gradually become smaller and smaller, though perhaps it would never vanish altogether.

What shall we say of the sceptical interpretation of 'the fear of the Lord is the beginning of wisdom'? The essential point about it is that 'the beginning' is taken to mean '*only* the beginning'. According to this interpretation there is not really any Lord to be feared, or at any rate we have no good reason for believing that there is. Nevertheless, anthropomorphic ways of thinking—or perhaps we should say 'animistic' ones— are congenial to immature minds. At that stage of our mental development (and some of us never grow out of it) the concept of the Moral Law is altogether too abstract for us to grasp. It must therefore be personified in the form of a superhuman being who tells us what we are to do and what we are not to do, and moreover rewards us when we obey him and punishes us when we disobey him. But those of us who do eventually manage to reach a state of intellectual maturity will then see for ourselves that the actions which this imaginary being was supposed to command are in fact right, and those which he was supposed to forbid are in fact wrong: and then we shall be able to dispense with the 'theological utilitarianism' which the author or authors of Proverbs accepted.

A 'THEOLOGICAL FOUNDATION' FOR MORALITY

In the sceptical view which we have just been considering
the fear of the Lord is a kind of temporary prop or support
for morally immature persons, which they can dispense with
when their moral education has been completed. The fear of
the Lord is the beginning of wisdom, but only the beginning.
When we are grown up, we shall come to see that right actions
are to be done for their own sake, no matter who commands
us to do them, and even though no one at all commands us
to do them. On this view, the theory which defines 'right' as
'what God commands us to do', and 'wrong' as 'what God
forbids us to do' is just a kind of *Interimsethik*.

But there are some who give it a much more exalted status
than that. They think that morality really does have 'a theological foundation' and that if there were no God, nothing
would be either right or wrong. The only way of settling the
question 'Is it right to do this?' is to consult the Divine Statute
Book, so to speak. Indeed, if there were no such statute book,
the question 'Is it right to do this?' could not even be asked.
And where shall we find the statute book? In the Bible perhaps, or in the teachings of the Church. Or perhaps it is also
written (not always very legibly) in our own consciences. But
even if it is, *we* did not write it, by using our own moral discernment, for on this view we have no such discernment. This
private statute book, if we do indeed possess it, was written
by the finger of God.

I wish to suggest, however, that the whole idea of providing
morality with a 'theological foundation' is a mistake, and
moreover a grave disservice to theology itself; and not only
to Christian theology, but to any theology of the theistic kind.
One of the consequences would be that the term 'ethical
theism' was just a meaningless pleonasm, equivalent to 'theistic
theism'.

Let us consider the proposition 'God is righteous'. What
kind of a proposition is this? How could a logician classify it?
Is it an analytic proposition, true by definition, like '$2+1=3$'?

Or is it a synthetic proposition, like 'The Mayor of Winterbourne Magna is righteous'? (There could conceivably be an unrighteous Mayor of Winterbourne Magna, even though there never has been.)

We notice, however, that the word 'God' can be used as a proper name, and is so used in the language of religious devotion: and it is not clear whether the distinction between analytic and synthetic applies to a proposition whose subject is a proper name. So let us substitute a descriptive phrase for the word 'God' and say 'the Lord of All is righteous'. Is this proposition synthetic or analytic? To discover what the logical character of a proposition is, the best plan is to consider what we should be doing if we denied it. There are, however, two ways of denying that the Lord of All is righteous. (1) One might say 'there is no Lord of All', and then the question whether he was righteous would not arise. (2) Or one might agree that there is such a being but deny that he is righteous. What we have to discuss is this second way of denying the proposition, and we have to ask what kind of denial it would be. Any theist would certainly maintain that it is a mistake to deny the Lord's righteousness, but what kind of a mistake does he think it is? Is it a mistake concerning a matter of fact, like denying the righteousness of Socrates? Or is it an absurdity, like denying that a square object has four corners or denying that a red thing is coloured?

To put it in another way: if we believe that there is a being who is the Lord of All but deny that he is righteous, is this supposed to be a logical mistake, a 'conceptual muddle'? Or is it supposed to be a factual mistake—no doubt an important one, because of the effect it has on our personal lives—but still not at all the same thing as it would be to say that a red thing is colourless? Does a theist think it just happens to be true that the Lord of All is also righteous, as it happens to be true that two Roman emperors were also philosophers?[1]

[1] Marcus Aurelius and Julian.

THE DEVELOPMENT OF THE CONCEPT OF DEITY

I find this question very difficult, and suggest that it can only be answered by taking a somewhat circuitous route. The world-outlook which we now call theism did not come into existence full-grown, as it were, as the goddess Athene is supposed to have done when she was born from the head of Zeus. It grew up gradually over a long period of time: and in theistic religion as elsewhere a proposition which was taken at first to be synthetic may later come to be regarded as analytic.

The process which we have to consider is the gradual development of the *concept* of Deity; and let us tentatively divide this process into five stages.

1. The first stage is just the belief that there is a very powerful conscious being whom we call 'God' or 'The Lord of All'.

2. Next, we come to believe also that there are no limits to his power. At that stage the proposition 'God is omnipotent' is synthetic.

3. But gradually this too comes to be part of what we *mean* by the word 'God': omnipotence comes to be included in the *concept* of Deity, and then 'God is omnipotent' becomes an analytic proposition.

4. Later still, it comes to be thought that God is not only omnipotent but also perfectly righteous. At that stage 'God is perfectly righteous' was a synthetic proposition: an important piece of 'news', as it were, which was brought to us by the Old Testament prophets.

5. But gradually this too comes to be part of the meaning of the word 'God' and then 'God is perfectly righteous' becomes an analytic proposition.

What does *not* become analytic at any stage of this process is the proposition 'God exists'. At any rate, I shall assume that no existential proposition is analytic. So in order to avoid misunderstandings, let me re-formulate the two analytic propositions I have mentioned. It is possible to express them in a conditional form: 'If there is a God, he is omnipotent' and 'if there is a God, he is perfectly righteous'. These do come to be analytic, true by definition, as the meaning of the word 'God' comes to be enriched, as it were, by the process of religious development. And yet they were not always analytic. There was a time when each of them was synthetic, a 'piece of news', and at each stage the concept of Deity became more complex but also (one might say) it came to be refined or purified. What began just as theism gradually turned into ethical theism. And this process of enrichment and refinement has gone further. That God is *merciful* as well as righteous is 'no news' to us, but one suspects that there was a time when it was 'news' to at least some of the people of Israel. That God is love was news indeed, a very important part of the 'good news' of the Gospel. But unfortunately we have become so accustomed to it that we no longer notice what an astonishing piece of news it is. It has indeed been incorporated, as it were, into the Christian concept of God, but perhaps this happened too easily; and many of us have forgotten that 'good news' is the literal meaning of the word 'Gospel' (εὐαγγέλιον).

Now let us return to the question we were trying to answer: Is it a logical mistake (a 'conceptual muddle') to assert that there is a Lord of All but deny that he is righteous, or is it a factual mistake? Or rather, which sort of mistake does a theist think it is?

We can see now that one cannot give 'a straight answer' to this question. At an early stage in the development of the theistic concept of Deity, it was a factual mistake to deny that the Lord of All is righteous. There was a stage at which it was 'news' that he is righteous: a piece of news which was at once terrifying and wonderful. But gradually this idea of the Lord's righteousness came to be included within the theistic concept of Deity; it came to be part of what theists mean by the word 'divine'; and from that time onwards it has been, and still is, a logical mistake, a conceptual muddle, to deny that the Lord of All is righteous. At any rate that is how the theist himself would put it. But an atheist too, or an agnostic, must agree that *within* the fully developed theistic world-outlook it is a conceptual mistake (not just a factual mistake) to deny that the Lord of All is righteous; and therefore any theists who say 'The Lord of All might conceivably not have been righteous, though as a matter of fact he is' must be misunderstanding the theory or world-outlook which they themselves claim to accept.

MORALITY AND DIVINE COMMANDS

What bearing does this have on the idea of providing morality with a 'theological foundation'? And what kind of a theological foundation would it be? The most obvious plan is to define 'right' and 'wrong' in terms of God's commands. At quite an early stage in the development of theism, it came to be thought that God is righteous; and before long this came to be part of the meaning of the word 'divine' as theists use it. And then it might seem an obvious step to go further and maintain that the word 'right' just *means* 'what God commands us to do' and 'wrong' just *means* 'what God forbids us to do'. There are also some actions which are morally indifferent, neither right nor wrong. It is neither right nor wrong to wear a bow-tie every Saturday. We may indeed say that I 'have a right' to do so if I like, and it follows from this that other people would be doing wrong if they tried to stop me.

It is an important fact that there are many actions which are neither right nor wrong, and I am inclined to think that moralists have not paid sufficient attention to it. It has a close connection with the concept of liberty. An action which is neither right nor wrong is one which we are 'at liberty' to do or not to do, as we please. On the view I am now trying to state (in order to show how paradoxical it is) an action of this kind would be one which God neither commands nor forbids; but since it is so fortunate for all of us that there are many actions which he neither commands nor forbids, he does perhaps command us to thank him for it. Surely we should be thankful that we do sometimes have what is called 'a moral holiday'?

C

But what do we mean by the word 'commandment'? 'Dixitque Deus: Fiat lux, et facta est lux' (Genesis 1: 3). Was this a command, a command which was instantaneously obeyed? No, for it was not addressed to anyone. Indeed, at that stage there was no one to be commanded. It was just an act of omnipotence; and though we may call it good, and think of it as a manifestation of creative love, we cannot call it righteous. So far as I can see, the concept of righteousness only becomes relevant when there are conscious creatures, capable of happiness or misery. But at that stage, according to the Genesis story, there were no conscious creatures of any kind, and the only conscious being was the Creator himself. We can only speak of commands when there are conscious creatures to be commanded. They must also be in some degree intelligent creatures. They must be capable of understanding what it is that they are told to do.

Moreover, in ordinary inter-human commands there is always some ignorance in the mind of the person who gives the command. He cannot know, though he may believe, that you will in fact do what he tells you to do. Conceivably it is not in your power to do it. And even though it is in your power, you may prefer to suffer the consequences of disobedience. It follows from this that for an omniscient being commanding would be something different from what it is for us, since he would know beforehand whether his command was going to be obeyed or not. There is, as it were, something tentative about human commands. You may hope that the other person will do what you tell him to do, and it may be a confident hope. But hope is incompatible with knowledge. If you know that something is going to happen you cannot hope that it is going to happen, though you may anticipate it with pleasure. The schoolmaster tried to overcome the difficulty about the tentativeness of human commands when he said to the boys, 'Stand up, or if you won't, then don't stand up; I *will* be obeyed.' But he was not very successful. He only succeeded in making his command tautologous, and thereby it ceased to be a command at all. That someone does what he is commanded to do is always a synthetic proposition. It might conceivably have been false, even though it is in fact true.

If this analysis of the concept of 'a commandment' is correct, what shall we say of the theory that 'right' and 'wrong', in the moral sense of those words, are to be defined in terms of God's commands? On that view 'it is right to help an injured person' would mean 'God commands us to help an injured person whenever it is in our power to do so'; and when we call someone a good man (in the moral sense of the word 'good') we should mean that he always obeys God's commands if it is in his power to do so. Or if we think this definition too exacting, perhaps we should say that he obeys them much more often than not if it is in his power to do so.

We should notice, however, that a good man need not know or even believe or even guess that he *is* obeying God's commands when he does what is right, or that he is disobeying them when he does what is wrong. Otherwise we should be committed to the conclusion that only theists are capable of doing right actions, or wrong ones either, and that no atheist or agnostic is either a good man or a bad man.

Another difficulty in this 'pious obedience' analysis of moral concepts, and an even more important one, is that we apply the word 'good' to God himself. Indeed, we say that he is wholly good, or good beyond comparison. But does it make sense to say that he obeys his own commandments? How can the notion of obedience be applied to the Lord of All?

I think we all feel that something has been omitted in this type of ethical theory. It is a 'reductionist' theory, an attempt to define moral concepts in terms of something other than themselves. That the Lord of All is wholly righteous is a proposition which no theist would deny. But is it just a tautology? Is it just another way of saying 'The Lord of All is the Lord of All'?

Moreover, no theist would deny that the Lord of All gives commands to his rational creatures. But if we go on to say that what he commands us to do is always right, are we just saying over again that there are actions which he commands us to do? Certainly not. We are saying something else and something important too, though how exactly it should be formulated is a matter of controversy between different ethical theories. We are at any rate expressing approval of what the Lord commands, whatever we may think the correct analysis of 'approval' is. And more than that: we are saying that we would disapprove of ourselves if we did not do what he commands and even that we would disapprove of anyone who was in the same circumstances as we are and failed to do what we are now commanded to do (anyone, for instance, who had made a promise and failed to keep that promise when it was in his power to do so).

All this is in a way platitudinous. It only amounts to saying that we ourselves are moral beings. A moral being is not merely one who obeys commands (no matter whose commands they are). He is one who has the rather awe-inspiring power of judging for himself whether an action is right or wrong. This, perhaps, is part of what we mean when we say that we are not only God's creatures, but also his 'children'.

2

PARANORMAL COGNITION, SYMBOLISM, AND INSPIRATION

THE remarks I shall make in this chapter are going to be very tentative and speculative. I shall often be saying things which I myself only half understand. These are deep waters, and I shall often be out of my depth. But unless we take the risk of sinking, we shall never learn to swim. I shall ask you to consider some very difficult questions which seem to me both interesting and important. But please do not attach too much importance to the answers which I shall suggest. My aim is to persuade you to think about these questions for yourselves, in the light of your own personal experience.

Let us begin by making the assumption that paranormal cognition is a two-stage process. In the first stage, something happens at an unconscious level of our personalities. We unconsciously receive a paranormal impression of some kind. Then, in the second stage, this paranormal impression emerges in one way or another into our consciousness. It is perfectly useless to us, unless and until it 'gets itself across' in one way or another into our conscious minds.

I say 'in one way or another', because the empirical evidence suggests that this process of emergence may take many different forms. For example, a paranormal impression may emerge in the form of a dream, or in the form of waking mental imagery, or in an intermediate form—something between a dream-image and an ordinary waking mental image—when we are in the 'twilight' state beween sleeping and waking. Again, it may emerge in the form of a vision or a voice, a visual or auditory hallucination. In some of the 'crisis apparitions' reported in the literature of psychical research a telepathically received impression seems to have 'emerged' in the form of a visual hallucination.

On the other hand, a paranormal impression may emerge in quite a different way, in the form of what is called 'a hunch'—an unreasoned belief which we suddenly find ourselves having. The belief is unreasoned in the sense that we are not aware of any evidence to support it, and yet it turns out to be correct. Probably we all know persons whose 'hunches' are surprisingly often correct, though they have no idea how their hunches come to them.

Again, a paranormally received impression may emerge in the form of an equally unreasoned impulse to do something: for instance, an impulse to go home at once or to write a letter to So-and-so, though there is no apparent reason for doing so. In a religious person it might take the form of an impulse to pray for somebody whom one has not thought of for months.

A paranormal impression may also emerge in the form of non-voluntary bodily behaviour, as in automatic writing, or in slips of the tongue, or in the automatic speech which occurs in the mediumistic trance. The superstitions of the Ancients about unintentionally saying 'ill-omened words' were not altogether groundless. An unconscious precognitive impression might emerge in that way. Such words might also reveal unconscious malevolent wishes in the mind of the speaker. In either case, it would be perfectly reasonable to pay some attention to them.

It is also possible that a paranormal impression may emerge when one *mishears* words uttered by another person. There is a celebrated example of this in the history of Ancient Rome. When Crassus and his army were marching through the streets of Rome in 53 B.C. on their way to Syria, there was a woman in the street who was selling figs to the soldiers as they passed by. The figs came from the Island of Caunos, and the woman shouted 'Cauneas, Cauneas' to advertise her wares. But this was misheard by the spectators as 'Cave ne eas', 'take care that you do not go'. The expedition ended in disaster. The

Roman army was defeated by the Parthians at the battle of Carrhae, and Crassus himself was killed a few days later.

One might describe this auditory experience, this mis-hearing of the fig-seller's words, as a partial hallucination by means of which an unconscious precognition manifested itself in the consciousness of the hearers. (There is a visual parallel for this in the use of the Rohrschach ink-blots.)

We may notice too that professional 'psychics' or 'sensitives' make use of rather similar methods for answering the questions which their clients ask them: for instance, gazing into a crystal ball, or looking at floating tea-leaves in a cup of tea. We may also consider the many different methods of 'divination' which have been practised in different ages and countries. It looks as if these curious procedures, which seem so very silly and pointless to modern Western people, were ways of inducing unconsciously-received paranormal impressions to emerge into consciousness; or, at least, this may explain how these curious methods came to be used long ago, though it may have been supposed later (quite wrongly) that they had some kind of 'magical' efficacy in themselves.

A 'CENSORSHIP'

Let us pause for a moment to reflect on this rather surprising fact that paranormally received impressions 'emerge' in so many different ways.

It looks as if there were some sort of obstacle or block-age which has to be overcome before a paranormal impression can emerge into consciousness: some kind of 'censorship', which tends to repress it or keep it out of consciousness. There might well be several different ways of overcoming or circumventing this censorship; which way is most effective might depend on the personal idiosyncracy of the percipient, or on the mental or bodily state in which he is at that particular time. We notice in this connection that other unconscious mental contents, unconscious wishes for example, tend to emerge most easily in dreams, or in the twilight state between sleeping and waking; or in the waking fantasies we have 'at the back of our minds' (in the margin of the field of consciousness when our attention is focused on something quite different); or again in 'slips of the tongue' or 'slips of the pen'. I am assuming here that the concepts developed by the Depth-Psychologists are relevant to the study of paranormal cognition: as they surely must be, if paranormal impressions are received at an unconscious level.

If so, there is nothing very paradoxical in the idea of a censorship or repressive mechanism which tends to prevent telepathic or clairvoyant or precognitive impressions from emerging into consciousness. From the point of view of the psychical researcher this censorship is of course an obstacle. Nevertheless, it might be very useful to the ordinary human being. In the first place, it might be biologically useful. In the vast majority of cases, the information we receive by means of our sense organs must have the first claim on our attention, if we are to adapt ourselves to our physical environment. We should not be very successful in adapting ourselves to it if paranormal impressions were constantly intruding, especially as they might easily be impressions about events which are quite remote in space or time or both.[1]

Moreover, it might well be that if someone's consciousness were flooded with paranormal impressions all the time, his personal identity would be disrupted. He might well be reduced to a kind of schizophrenic condition, because he would be unable to assimilate and make sense of such a heterogeneous multitude of data. The censorship or repressive mechanism I have mentioned might well be useful, or even indispensable, as a means of safeguarding the integrity of one's personality. The censor is our enemy in some ways, but perhaps he is our friend in others.

If there is any truth in what I have said, it is conceivable and even likely that many paranormal impressions never succeed in 'emerging' at all. It is even possible that at an

[1] Cf. below, p. 48.

unconscious level we are having them all the time. Again, among those which do succeed in emerging there may be many which are not recognized for what they are. Those 'casual' and 'irrelevant' thoughts and mental images which we often have—where do they come from? Do all of them come from one's own personal unconscious? Or do some of them come telepathically from the minds of other people?

SYMBOLISM

So far I have said nothing about symbolism. But we are now in a position to consider this rather difficult and elusive topic. It would be generally agreed that when paranormal impressions do succeed in emerging into consciousness, they often emerge in a symbolic form. That is true of other unconscious mental contents too (e.g. unconscious wishes, fears, and hatreds) and it is just what we should expect if what I have said about the 'censorship' is correct. By assuming a symbolic form, a paranormally received impression may contrive to get into consciousness when the censor would otherwise keep it out.

But the term 'symbol' is a somewhat slippery one. For instance, there is a subject called Symbolic Logic,[1] and the sense in which the word 'symbolic' is used there has very little connection with the one which now concerns us. What we have in mind, when we say that paranormal cognition is often symbolic, is the contrast between the symbolic and the literal.

In a dream, for example, your friend Mr. Postlethwaite might be symbolized by an image of a lion, because he has a lion-like temperament. The lion image does in a way represent him or stand for him, but it represents him in an oblique or indirect or non-literal manner. Quite an elaborate process of interpretation may be needed before you realize that this dream-image does stand for or represent that particular person.

[1] In Symbolic Logic letters of the alphabet (including the Greek alphabet) are substituted for words, and technical signs such as $\sim$ (for 'not') and $\supset$ (for 'implies') are also used.

It is an important fact about paranormal cognition that it is often 'symbolic' in this way. What emerges into consciousness, in a telepathic dream or vision for instance, need not directly and literally represent what one is paranormally aware of or 'in touch with' at the unconscious level. So a certain amount of interpretation is needed before we can say what it is that is being paranormally cognized; and it might well be that the percipient himself is just the person who finds it particularly difficult to interpret his dream or vision correctly. For the very reason why this 'symbolic' disguise had to be adopted by the paranormally acquired idea was that it could not get into his consciousness otherwise. 'Symbolism' (in this sense of the term) is a way of evading or circumventing the censorship which I mentioned earlier.

But paranormal cognition is not always 'symbolic' in this sense, and if it had been, one may doubt whether the very existence of paranormal cognition could have been established. For instance, let us consider the card-guessing experiments of Dr. Rhine, Dr. Soal, and others. Such experiments could not provide any evidence for the existence of paranormal cognition, unless the percipient did sufficiently often score a 'direct hit' on the target card. Each guess he makes is either wholly right or wholly wrong: and if a guess is right in a symbolic sense but wrong in a literal sense, it is not counted as a 'hit'.

It has been said sometimes that this 'hit or miss' character of the card-guessing method is one of its weaknesses: and it is true that we do need other methods of investigation as well, methods more congenial (if one may say so) to the unconscious level of the human mind. But my point at present is that the card-guessing method does produce positive results, which it could not do if paranormal cognition were *always* symbolic.

The same is true of spontaneous cases, telepathic dreams for example. We should have no reason for thinking that there were telepathic dreams at all, if there had not been cases where some person's dream-images corresponded in a quite straightforward and not at all 'symbolic' manner with some event or state of affairs which he did not know of in any normal way.

That applies to telepathic hallucinations too. For instance in one of Tyrrell's cases (he calls it 'the Pillow Case')[1] a lady woke early in the morning and saw on her pillow 'what appeared to be half a sheet of notepaper with the words written on it "Elsie was dying last night". There was only one person to whom the message could refer, and it turned out that she had in fact died during that night.' The piece of notepaper with the written words on it was a visual hallucination, conveying paranormally acquired information to the percipient's consciousness (no piece of paper was actually there in physical fact). But in the sense of the term 'symbolic' which now concerns us, there was nothing symbolic about these hallucinatory words. They were a direct and literal description of the paranormally cognized event.

So there are cases, both spontaneous cases and experimental ones, in which a paranormal impression does manage to get through into consciousness without any distortion or disguise. It may be significant in Tyrrell's case which I have quoted that the percipient had only just woken up. We may suppose that she was not yet wide awake and had not quite emerged from the intermediate 'twilight' state between sleep and full waking consciousness. It looks as if the 'censor' is less effective at such times than he is when one is fully awake.

But now we come to a type of case which shows how slippery this notion of 'symbolism' can be. If the general picture I am presenting to you is right—if paranormally acquired information has to overcome some sort of barrier or censorship in order to get into consciousness—we should expect that it would quite often get there in an inaccurate or distorted form. There is a type of telepathy experiment in which the percipient is asked to make a drawing of some object which the agent is thinking of or imagining. In one such experiment the object was a pair of scissors, and the percipient produced a drawing of two separate ovals with a vertical straight line beside them.

○ ○ |

[1] G. N. M. Tyrell, *Science and Psychical Phenomena* (Methuen, 1938), p. 24.

We are inclined to regard this as an imperfect or inaccurate 'hit'. All three parts of a schematic picture of the object are there in the drawing, but their spatial relations are wrong. Perhaps some people might wish to call this a 'symbolic' picture of a pair of scissors. But surely it is better and clearer, though less exciting, to say that it is inaccurate; correct in some ways, since there really are two oval parts and one more or less straight part in a pair of scissors, but incorrect in another way, because the spatial relations between these three parts are wrong.

Again, there are cases where the paranormally acquired information can only get into consciousness if it is combined or mixed in with other thoughts and images which are not paranormal at all. I take this to be a way of eluding the vigilance of the censor. A traveller who wants to get some forbidden object through the customs puts it among a lot of other perfectly innocent objects in his suitcase; and then perhaps the customs official will not notice it. In a similar way, a dream may be partly telepathic, while other features of it may just come from the dreamer's personal unconscious, his own personal memories or wishes. If these two elements in the dream, the telepathic part and the non-telepathic part, just stand side by side, as it were, or if there are two episodes in the dream, one telepathic and then another reproducing the dreamer's personal memories or wishes, one would hardly want to call this a case of 'symbolism'. The obvious thing to say is that such a dream is just a mixed one, partly telepathic and partly not.

Now we can state our problem in a frank and uncompromising way. Can we find some method of going behind these disguises, this 'protective colouring', as it were, which a paranormally acquired idea may have to adopt in order to get into consciousness? It is as if an uninvited guest could only get into the ballroom by wearing a mask. Otherwise the doorkeeper will stop him. But once he has got in, we must persuade him or compel him to take off his mask, so that we may see him as he really is. That is our problem. It is not only a problem for psychical researchers, but for others too, perhaps for everyone. Many of us, perhaps even all of us, may quite frequently receive paranormal impressions which can only get into our conscious minds in this disguised way. The disguise may be so effective that we quite fail to suspect that it *is* a disguise; and even if we do suspect that it is, we do not know how to find out what there is behind it. In this way, we fail to make any use of paranormal information which we do actually receive.

Furthermore (to continue this analogy) our visitor may well be in such an exhausted and enfeebled condition, after his encounter with the door-keeper, that he has not enough strength to come up and shake hands with his hostess, and she never notices that he has entered the ballroom at all. The paranormal impression does manage to get into consciousness, but only into the margin of consciousness, not into the focus. For a moment or two we are aware of it, but only *just* aware of it ('at the back of our minds', as we say), and then we forget about it altogether.

If I am right so far, there are various sorts of indirect or oblique presentation which occur in paranormal cognition, as they also do when other sorts of unconscious mental contents 'emerge' or 'rise to the surface'; and according to my hypothesis, these are ways of circumventing the censorship or repressive mechanism which tends to prevent unconsciously received paranormal impressions from reaching consciousness at all. This indirect or oblique presentation is what people have in mind when they say that paranormal cognition often takes a 'symbolic' form. But I think it is better to use more frank and uncompromising words, such as 'disguise' and 'substitute'. It is true, and important, that paranormal impressions do often emerge into consciousness in a disguised form; and if we put it in that way, we can see what our problem is. Can we find ways of penetrating behind these disguises, this 'protective colouring', as it were, which a paranormally acquired idea may have to assume in order to slip into consciousness? Perhaps we might get some useful hints from the methods which the Depth-Psychologists use for the interpretation of dreams and of abnormal behaviour.

The trouble with the word 'symbol' is that it is such a very elastic word. It has also come to be a kind of 'numinous' word, if one may say so, a word which is at once mysterious and uplifting. This does cause some distress to a sober-minded philosopher. But it is not at all surprising that the word 'symbol' should have acquired this quasi-numinous character. We should all agree that symbols play a large part in religious experience, and in the more profound sorts of aesthetic experience also—in the appreciation of tragic drama, for instance, or of lyrical poetry. This is rather distressing to an analytic philosopher who wants us to make our statements in plain literal prose ('Why can't you call a spade a spade?').

But there is an important difference between symbols of this kind and those which we are concerned with when we discuss paranormal cognition. What we become aware of in telepathy or clairvoyance or precognition *can* always be described in a perfectly literal and matter-of-fact way. The information may come to us in a symbolic manner, but the symbols can be 'decoded'. The information we have received can always be translated into literal prose.

With the symbols which are used in poetry and art, and in some forms of religious experience too, this sort of literal translation is often impossible. Something is being conveyed to us which can only be conveyed in a 'symbolic' manner. There are ideas, important ones too, which we can only receive in a symbolic way, at least in our present state of spiritual immaturity. We often have to be 'taught in parables'. We are not as yet able to verify these ideas directly. Perhaps saints or angels can. But we ourselves cannot as yet 'go behind' the symbols and translate them into plain and literal prose.

What we do with them is rather to 'feed upon them', so to speak, to ruminate on them or meditate on them, and hope thereby to grow in insight. But that is not at all what we do with the images which come into our minds when we have a telepathic or clairvoyant or precognitive experience. Their function is to convey information about some plain matter of empirical fact (for example the fact that Mr. So-and-so is ill, or that a missing document is underneath a lot of handker-chiefs in such-and-such a drawer in the bedroom).

THE CONTROL OF PARANORMAL POWERS

This brings me to the next point which I wish to submit to you. It has sometimes been suggested that what Psychical Research is most in need of at present is a method of making paranormal powers controllable, so that we can use them at will, whenever we need them. At first sight this problem might seem insoluble. If these powers belong to the uncon-scious stratum of our personalities, how can we do anything to bring them under conscious and voluntary control? 'The spirit bloweth where it listeth.' But what we could conceivably do, by an exercise of conscious intelligence and will, is to provide the conditions in which the results of these uncon-scious operations can emerge into consciousness more easily. We might find a way of 'smoothing the passage', so to speak, between the unconscious level of our personalities and the conscious level. This may indeed be a difficult task (or should we say, a delicate task?) but I do not think it is an impossible one.

'INSPIRATION'

Let me mention a more or less parallel case. Every writer knows that when he writes a book or even a short essay, the 'creative' part of the work is done outside of consciousness. He cannot get on at all unless appropriate ideas just 'come' to him (consider such phrases as 'it occurred to me that . . .', 'it suddenly struck me that . . .'). He must just wait for them to occur to him. He does not construct them for himself by conscious effort. Much conscious effort may be needed afterwards in selecting among the ideas which 'come to him'. Some of them turn out to be irrelevant, and have to be rejected altogether; and those which do seem relevant have to be arranged in a logical order, and we have to consider what their consequences are. But fundamentally the process just depends on 'inspiration'; without this, the conscious intellectual machinery has nothing to work upon. 'Inspiration' is only a rather grand word for appropriate ideas which just 'come to us' or 'occur to us'. They come into consciousness as the result of unconscious mental operations.

But although these operations go on 'behind the scenes', as it were, we can do something to set them going, and to open our conscious minds to the results when the results are ready. For instance, you may suggest to yourself, just before going to sleep, that thoughts about such and such a topic will occur to you at 10 o'clock tomorrow morning, when you sit down to begin upon the draft of the next chapter. You turn the topic over in your mind before you go to sleep: not in full detail, because at present you are not clear about it, and a clear and detailed exposition of it is just what you cannot manage now, but hope to accomplish later. You just give a brief glance at the main points, as it were, and then go to sleep.

When the next morning comes, you will probably find that it is important to be punctual (it looks as if the unconscious were a good time-keeper). If 10 a.m. is the time specified, then at 10 a.m. you must be sure to be sitting at your writing-table with a pen or pencil in your hand and paper to write on. If something prevents you from doing this—a telephone call, for instance—the ideas you hoped for will not come.

Moreover, at the time when you are making the suggestion to yourself the night before, a certain tranquil confidence is needed—faith, if you like to call it so. Anxiety and fussiness are likely to have an inhibiting effect, because if you are anxious or fussy you are suggesting to yourself that you will fail. But when the tranquil confidence is there, one finds (at least usually) that this curious procedure works quite well. At any rate, it works well enough and often enough to make it worth using.

There is another little dodge which seems to make it work better. It is helpful to say to oneself while one is dressing or having breakfast, 'I wonder what the ideas will be which will come to me at 10 o'clock: at present I do not know at all what they are going to be, and won't it be rather exciting to see what they are? It is something to look forward to.' This is a way of strengthening the expectation—the faith, if you like—that appropriate ideas *are* going to come at the hour which you specified. For faith of this kind (like faith of other kinds) is something which can be cultivated. But here again one must not be fussy or anxious. A tranquil confidence is what is needed. The notion of 'hoisting oneself by one's own boot-straps' by a prodigious voluntary effort is just the wrong one.

I feel sure that very many intellectual workers use methods something like these for getting inspiration, though in detail one person's method may differ from another person's.

SOME VIEWS OF THE ANCIENTS

Do these remarks about 'inspiration' throw any light on the problem of bringing our paranormal powers under voluntary control? Could we say that conscious paranormal cognition is just a special case of 'receiving inspiration'? It is rather interesting to notice that the Ancients thought there was a close connection between the two. In classical Latin a poet is some- times called a *vates*, and this word also means 'a prophet' or a 'seer'. It is true that our word 'poet' (from the Greek ποιητής) literally means 'a maker'. But the Ancients were well aware that most of this 'making' has to occur outside the poet's consciousness, at any rate if his poem is going to be worth reading. As you will remember, the Ancients thought that there were supernatural beings called 'the Muses', and it was supposed to be one of these who put the words into the poet's mouth: somewhat as the god Apollo was supposed to put words into the mouth of the Delphic priestess when she made her prophecies or gave advice to the people who came to consult her.[1]

It seems to me that the Ancients were wise—wiser than they knew—when they expressed such views. It might be too much to say that paranormal cognition is just a special case of 'inspiration'. But the two things do have a good deal in common. In both cases something 'just comes to' a person, and in both it comes from some source which is outside his conscious mind. Again, in both cases it is usually necessary to take steps beforehand to 'smooth the passage' between the unconscious level of one's personality and the conscious level. Moreover, in both cases, you must be willing to receive what 'comes to you' and willing to pay some attention to it when it does come. It is as if someone else—or at any rate something other than your conscious self—were giving you something. And it takes two to make a gift. You cannot give me something unless I am willing to receive it; and many of us, I suspect, are *not* willing to receive what the unconscious part of our personality is offering to us. As I have suggested already, there may be many paranormal impressions at the unconscious level of our personality which never succeed in getting into consciousness at all; and those which do may have to disguise themselves first, in order to get past the censor. But not all of them are disguised; and in some of those which are, the disguise is pretty thin. By just making your mind a blank for a moment, you might find that the right interpretation occurred to you almost at once.

Unfortunately, many of us, I suspect, are a little afraid of the things which our own unconscious is trying to convey to us. No doubt we have some reason to be afraid. There are some pretty unpleasant things lurking there, in the unconscious region of our minds, if the Depth-Psychologists are right. But if we are too frightened of what the contents of the unconscious level of our personality may reveal to us, we shall

---

[1] On the paranormal powers of the Delphic priestess, see Frederick Myers's essay on the Delphic Oracle in his book *Essays, Classical*.

never succeed in making any use of the paranormal impressions we receive, and shall not even be aware that we have received them; and if they do occasionally manage to emerge into consciousness, we shall not try to penetrate behind the disguises which they often have to assume in order to get there. Moreover, when they emerge without any disguise, or with very little (as they sometimes do) we shall pay no attention to them and forget all about them a few moments afterwards.

MIRACLES AND THE PARANORMAL

In these lectures I have been trying to show that Psychical Research has some relevance to the Philosophy of Religion. No doubt it would be a great mistake to identify the paranormal with the spiritual. To take an extreme example, a mystical experience of 'union with God' is very different indeed from a telepathic dream. Both of them are 'beyond the normal'. But they are beyond it in quite different ways.

Nevertheless, there is an overlap between these two types of inquiry, the investigation of paranormal phenomena on the one hand, and the investigation of religious experience on the other. For instance, the 'good news' of the Christian Gospel is concerned, among other things, with life after death; and life after death is a subject on which psychical researchers have something to say.

Again, a psychical researcher does not use the word 'miracle'; but some of the phenomena which a religious person calls 'miraculous' do fall within the psychical researcher's field of interest, and can be explained in terms of telepathy or clairvoyance or telekinesis.

We must remember too that the impression which Jesus himself made on his contemporaries was concerned not only with what he said ('Never man so spake') but also with what he did ('He went about doing good'). He healed the sick and enabled some of his disciples to do the same. Unfortunately, paranormal healing is a subject which I am not competent to discuss. I cannot venture to offer any opinion on the scope and limits of what is now called 'psychosomatic medicine'. But if we try to imagine what impression the Gospels would make on an intelligent adult who had never read them or heard of them before, and now reads them for the first time, I think he would be astonished to notice the importance attached to one very strange type of healing, the casting out of devils or demons. It looks as if the psychological disorders which we now call 'dissociated personality' and 'alternating personality' were very common in Palestine at that time; and when Jesus 'went about doing good', the good that he did was often the healing of personality disorders of this kind.

It is unfortunate that the word 'miracle' has been devalued for us by David Hume's celebrated essay on the subject.[1] He has persuaded many of us to think that the word 'miracle' just means 'an event which is inconsistent with causal laws'. But all it meant originally was 'a wonder', a surprising or extraordinary event. In the New Testament itself the miracles of Jesus are sometimes called 'signs' ($\sigma\eta\mu\epsilon\hat{\iota}\alpha$). Signs of what? Signs, presumably, of more than normal human powers. But so far as I can see, there is no suggestion in the Gospels that miraculous events or actions were somehow violations of causal laws. The New Testament writers did not think in such terms. To them, the idea of 'a causal law', which modern Europeans acquired in the seventeenth and eighteenth centuries, was something quite unfamiliar. Moreover, we ourselves are beginning to have some doubts about it, at least so far as microphysical events are concerned. It looks as if the laws of Nature, at any rate the laws of Physics, the most fundamental of all the Natural Sciences, are turning out to be no more—and no less—than statistical regularities.

[1] In *Essays, Moral, Political and Literary*, p. 517 (Oxford edition).

3

PETITIONARY PRAYER AND
TELEPATHY

In this chapter I shall not say anything about mystical prayer, nor about what is called the prayer of adoration. Far be it from me to suggest that either of them is unimportant. But I shall only be concerned with petitionary prayer, the sort of prayer which is referred to in the words 'Ask and ye shall receive'. It seems to me that the practice of petitionary prayer raises difficult theoretical problems which are not very often discussed.

Let us begin by considering petitionary prayer on behalf of others. We should all agree that it is good to wish well to others. We do not usually suppose that this well-wishing benefits them in any direct way. But it does have an effect on the well-wishing person himself. It makes him more likely to help them effectively, if any opportunity of helping them arises. He is also more likely to notice such opportunities when they come. He is as it were 'on the look out' for them.

WELL-WISHING AND WISHFUL THINKING

A person who is at once kind-hearted and irreligious (and there are many who are both) might therefore think that there is something to be said for the practice of petitionary prayer, at any rate when one prays on behalf of other people. He might regard it as a voluntary exercise in well-wishing. In order to offer such a prayer, you do have to think as clearly as you can about the needs of the other person, the troubles by which he is afflicted, the dangers or difficulties which confront him. You have to take an interest in him, a benevolent attitude, and a well-informed one, as well-informed as you can make it. Of course our irreligious but kind-hearted friend does not believe that these thoughtful prayers or prayerful thoughts make any difference at all to the person for whom you are praying. But they may well make *you* into a more benevolent person, and a more effectively benevolent person, just because they get you into the habit of thinking both carefully and kindly about the needs and the troubles of other people.

Moreover, an unreligious person, if he has reason to think that other people are praying for him, can quite consistently be grateful to them for doing so. He rejects their theology, but he can sincerely thank them for their benevolence. He may also concede that their theology, however unacceptable it is to him, does nevertheless provide them with a useful psychological technique for maintaining and increasing their own benevolence. He might even envy them for having this ready-made technique at their disposal. But intellectual honesty forbids him to use this psychological technique himself, though he can and does approve warmly of the well-wishing which it facilitates. He will point out that well-wishing is one thing, but wishful thinking is another, and will add that, unfortunately, petitionary prayer is a mixture of both.

There is some difficulty in this distinction between well-wishing and wishful thinking. For wishing itself contains thinking; at any rate conscious wishing does. If I wish that next Sunday will be a fine day, I have to think or conceive of next Sunday as a day which is going to be fine. If I wish you a happy journey I must think of you as one who is going to have a happy journey. Indeed, conscious desire could quite well be described as optative thinking ('May you have a happy journey').

But this thinking of A *as* B, or *as* going to be B, must be carefully distinguished from believing that A *is* B or *is* going to be B. In the terminology of some philosophers, thinking of A as B is called 'the entertaining of a proposition'. We cannot assent to a proposition without entertaining it, but we can very well entertain it without assenting to it. Indeed, we have to entertain it in order to doubt it or reject it. This attitude of entertaining a proposition is a necessary constituent of desire also, or at any rate of conscious desire. If I desire another cup of tea I entertain the proposition 'I am going to have another cup of tea', though I need not believe it. The same applies to aversion. If I am averse from going to London tomorrow I have to entertain the proposition 'I am going to London tomorrow', though perhaps my aversion will be soon so great that I shall never go there again.

There is a sense, then, in which well-wishing, and ill-wishing too, could quite well be described as 'wishful thinking', at any rate if our wish is a conscious one. But the phrase 'wishful thinking', as it is commonly used, means something different, namely wishful *believing*: believing some proposition merely because one wishes it to be true, regardless of the strength or weakness of the evidence for it. That is why our kind-hearted but unreligious friend has this ambivalent attitude to the practice of petitionary prayer.

In so far as petitionary prayer is an exercise in well-wishing, he warmly approves of it. It is good that everyone should do all he can to make himself into a benevolent person. A community of mutually well-wishing persons is better than a community of mutually indifferent ones, where nobody takes any interest in the welfare of his neighbours; and *a fortiori* it is vastly better than a community of mutually ill-wishing ones. But unfortunately petitionary prayer, at any rate in theistic religions,[1] contains wishful believing as well: the belief that there is a Supreme Being, the Lord of All, who loves every one of us, and the belief, moreover, that he 'hears' and 'answers' our prayers. What evidence could there be for such extraordinary beliefs? But unfortunately these wishful beliefs are an essential part of the psychological technique which these religious persons use in their well-wishing exercises. No doubt

---

[1] In Hinayana Buddhism, petitionary prayer is presumably replaced by conscious and deliberate well-wishing.

this technique is an effective one for those who can use it. The *idea* of a loving, omniscient and omnipotent being has a psychological power which we must not under-estimate. But surely the belief that there actually *is* such a being cannot be anything but a wishful one?

'ASK AND YE SHALL RECEIVE'

Nevertheless, a religious person will obstinately maintain that his prayers are quite frequently answered. He may even add that when they seem not to be, it sometimes turns out later that he has received something *better* than he asked. His view is that we may safely rely on the Gospel saying 'Ask and ye shall receive'.

Let us consider this saying 'Ask and ye shall receive', which is attributed to Jesus himself. I hope the reader will not think me profane if I first make some remarks on its logical properties. 'Ask and ye shall receive' is both an injunction and a statement. There is nothing very unusual or paradoxical in this combination. Other examples of it are 'Press the button and the bell will ring', 'Run, and you will catch the train'.

'Ask and ye shall receive' may be paraphrased thus: 'If you ask, you will receive; therefore, ask'. The imperative 'ask' cannot be verified or falsified. It is neither true nor false. With an imperative, the only alternatives are to do what is commanded or to refrain from doing it. But the conditional statement 'If you ask, you will receive' *is* true or false.

In just the same way the imperative 'press the button' is neither true nor false, but 'if you press the button, the bell will ring' *is* true or false; and if you wish to find out which it is, the simplest plan is to press the button. Indeed, when you say to me 'Press the button and the bell will ring', it almost seems that you are inviting me to find out for myself whether your conditional prediction is true. And if you say 'Run, and you will catch the train' you are doing something more. You are recommending me or urging me to run, because you assume that I wish to catch it. The same applies to 'Ask and ye shall receive'. It is assumed that we wish to receive what we ask for.

There is one other logical point which is worth mentioning. It is *not* said that asking is a necessary condition for receiving, but only that it is a sufficient condition. If asking were a necessary condition for receiving, the appropriate formulation would have been 'You will not receive unless you ask' or 'Refrain from asking, and you will not receive'. But no religious person would think that asking is a necessary condition for receiving. He would say that we receive many things from God without asking for them. We may find, to our dismay, that we are not very thankful to him for these unasked blessings. But then we may ask, and receive, his grace to enable us to be so.

PRO INSIPIENTE

A book was once written called *Liber pro insipiente*. It was a criticism of St. Anselm's version of the Ontological Argument for the existence of God; and the *insipiens* was the man referred to in Psalm 13, 'Dixit insipiens in corde suo "Non est Deus" ' —'the fool hath said in his heart "There is no God" '. I shall try to state the view he might take about the phenomena of petitionary prayer. My *insipiens*, however, does not go so far as to say 'Non est Deus'. Instead, he says that the phenomena of petitionary prayer give no support to the proposition 'Deus est'. He is an agnostic, not an atheist. To put it very crudely, he admits that petitionary prayer 'works' and offers a non-theistic explanation of 'how it works'.

His first step is to remind us that there are two different sorts of good which a religious person may ask for when he prays. He may pray for himself, on his own behalf. He may ask for strength or courage or intellectual enlightenment. If he is confronted by some problem, practical or theoretical, which he cannot solve by his own unaided efforts, he may pray that he may be shown how to solve it. Again, he may ask that he himself may be delivered from some danger, for instance when he has lost his way among rocks on a mountain-top, because a cloud has come down and he cannot see more than a yard or two ahead. In such cases, the 'good' he asks for is his own, or will be if he receives it.

But he may also pray for others. Then he asks that *they* may receive the help or guidance or healing which they need. So far as I can see, both kinds of prayer are recommended in the saying 'Ask and ye shall receive'. At any rate, it is certainly not said that we shall only receive when we ask on another person's behalf, despite the 'altruistic' character of Christian teaching.

PRAYER AND SELF-SUGGESTION

My *insipiens*, however, is a much more sophisticated person than the one of whom the Psalmist spoke. First, he will draw our attention to the phenomena of self-suggestion. He will say that when we pray to God on our own behalf and ask that we may be given the courage or strength or intellectual enlightenment we need, we do quite often receive what we prayed for. But surely this can be explained by self-suggestion? It is true that the *idea* of God plays an important part in the process; but what reason is there to think that God himself has anything to do with it, if indeed there is such a being? The idea of God is just part of the psychological machinery which the praying person uses: its function is to make the self-suggestion more confident by 'personifying' our own unconscious powers.

Secondly, the *insipiens* will also remind us that the suggestions which we make to ourselves should be positive rather than negative. It would be a mistake to suggest to yourself 'I am *not* going to be frightened' or 'I am not going to lose my temper when So-and-so comes to see me' or 'I am not going to get stuck in the piece of writing I have to do tomorrow morning'. It has been said that 'the unconscious does not understand the word "not"'.

This, I think, is a rather mythical way of expressing a logical truth, and pointing out that it has important consequences which we should bear in mind, when we consider how we should conduct our thoughts. The logical truth is just that 'not-*p*' is equivalent to '*p* is false'. So if you think to yourself 'I am not going to be frightened' you also have the thought 'I *am* going to be frightened' although you reject it; or rather, you must have it in order to reject it. If some of our thoughts about ourselves have a tendency to verify themselves (and that is what self-suggestion amounts to) they will only have it if they are single-minded.

For the same reason, it would be a mistake to suggest to oneself before some troublesome interview 'I am going to keep my temper' and then add 'But of course it will be difficult, and perhaps I shall not be able to manage it'. One writer on this subject has even referred to a 'law of reversed effort'. His point was, I think, that if one makes one's self-suggestion in an effortful manner, one is *ipso facto* thinking of the possibility of failure, and thereby suggesting to oneself that one will in fact fail.

It might seem that there is a kind of conflict here between single-mindedness and intellectual honesty. Surely there is very good empirical evidence for the proposition 'if one resolves to keep one's temper, one often fails to keep it'? So it is quite likely, even more likely than not, that I shall fail again this time. If I am an intellectually honest person, what right have I to disregard this unpleasant possibility or even probability?

The answer to this difficulty is that, though self-suggestions do refer to the future, they are not just forecasts or rational predictions, as when I predict that I shall miss the train because the bus to the station is twenty minutes late. A person who uses self-suggestion is indeed *thinking* of the future (his own future) but he is not trying to make a rational prediction about what it will be. His aim is quite different. His aim is to bring about one sort of future event rather than another.

If one is making a rational prediction (a weather forecast, for example) one must consider several alternative possibilities, together with the evidence for, and against, each of them. That is just what we do *not* do when we use self-suggestion. Instead, we fix our attention on just one alternative, for instance 'I am going to speak kindly to him when he comes' and avert our attention from other equally possible alternatives—speaking coldly or angrily or just glaring at him and saying nothing at all. This sort of single-mindedness is not always easily achieved; but when we do manage to achieve it, it usually has the desired effect.

LIMITATIONS OF THE SELF-SUGGESTION THEORY OF PRAYER

But whatever we think of this self-suggestion theory of petitionary prayer, it will only apply, at the best, to the prayers which a person makes on his own behalf. Moreover, we notice that even when a person prays on his own behalf, and his prayer is answered, the answer often comes about through the actions of other people.

Suppose that you have promised to visit a friend in a town you have never been to before, and you get lost. It is Sunday evening and pouring with rain. There is no one about in the streets. You have no map of the town, or if you have, you forgot to bring it with you. All you know is that your friend's address is No. 15 Acacia Street. Then, if you are a very pious person, you may ask for God's help. 'Please, Lord, may I find Tom's house.'

There is indeed a tradition that when a person prays on his own behalf, he must ask only for 'spiritual' goods and not for 'temporal' ones, although when one is praying for another person one may ask for goods of either sort on his behalf. I doubt whether this tradition is supported by what we are told about prayer in the New Testament, but let us suppose that you accept it. Still, you did promise to visit your friend Tom this evening, and keeping one's promise presumably counts as a 'spiritual' good. So you have no scruples about making this petition. And then a few minutes later you see someone opening his front door to let the cat out. You ask him where Acacia Street is. He tells you to take the first turning on the right, and then the third turning on the left, and you get to your friend's house no more than ten minutes late.

THE 'MIRACULOUS' THEORY OF ANSWERS TO PRAYER

Was it just a coincidence that the man happened to let the cat out at that particular time? Conceivably it might be. But one should consider a remark made by Archbishop Temple: 'When I pray, coincidences begin to happen.' This seems to me a good way of stating the problem. Any one case in which a person receives what he prays for might be a coincidence. But if this sort of thing happens quite frequently in the lives of persons who pray (and the testimony of religious people is that it does) here is a fact which needs explanation.

What could the explanation be? Are we to say that when you received what you asked for, this came about by a kind of *ad hoc* divine intervention, whereby the man was 'made' to let the cat out just at the time when you were passing, though he would not otherwise have done so? Or perhaps you were 'made' to walk at such a speed that you would reach the spot just when the cat was being let out?

This might be described as the 'miraculous' theory of the way petitionary prayers are answered. It would amount to saying that God works a kind of minor miracle on the praying person's behalf. I do not wish to maintain that miracles never happen. But if one may venture to say so, they would cease to be miraculous if they happened all day and every day. A miracle is by definition something exceptional, 'extraordinary' in the literal sense of the word; and this is still true if the miracle is, so to speak, a very little one.

Again, if someone prays to keep his temper during a difficult interview, and does somehow or other manage to keep it, are we to say that the laws of psychology are temporarily suspended for his benefit? Or if you pray that someone who is very ill may recover, and he does recover, are some of the laws of physiology suspended at your request?

It seems to me better, and indeed more consonant with a theistic view of the world, to say that we should revise our views of what the laws of nature are. And *a fortiori* that is the line which an irreligious person must take. It will be remembered that I am still speaking *pro insipiente*, and the question I am asking is, can he give a non-theistic explanation of the fact that petitionary prayers are often answered? For that is his aim: to give a non-theistic answer to the question 'what is the *modus operandi* of petitionary prayer?'.

We can now see that the phenomena of self-suggestion, important as they are, will not give the *insipiens* all he wants. At the very most, they will only enable him to explain how prayers on one's own behalf are answered, and not even all of these. For as I have pointed out already, when one prays for help for oneself, and receives it, the help may very well come through the actions of other people.

It seems to me, then, that the *insipiens* (who may well be a very learned person) had better take some account of the phenomena investigated by psychical researchers, para-normal or parapsychological phenomena. The most relevant of these, and perhaps the best established, is telepathy. So let us consider what bearing the phenomena of telepathy have on the question he is trying to answer.

TELEPATHY

The term 'telepathy' (literally 'feeling at a distance') was first used by F. W. H. Myers in 1882. His definition of it was 'the communication of impressions of any kind from one mind to another independently of the recognized channels of sense'; and the person *from* whom the impression comes is called by Myers 'the agent', while the person *to* whom it comes is called 'the percipient'.

These definitions, though they are still commonly used, need some comment, and perhaps some criticism.

First, we must consider the phrase 'impressions of any kind'. What is communicated need not be a piece of information, though it sometimes is. Instead, it might be an emotion, for instance fear or anxiety, or again, affection or love. Secondly, there is some difficulty about the word 'agent'. It suggests that the person from whom the communication comes is *doing* something. Sometimes this is true. At any rate, the person from whom the communication comes may wish that a certain other person shall receive it; and in the spontaneous cases (as opposed to the experimental ones) there is often an emotional link between the two persons. But it is not always true that the agent has a wish of this kind. Sometimes telepathy looks more like an involuntary or non-voluntary 'leakage' of some idea or emotion from one person's mind into another person's mind.

Thirdly, Myers's term 'percipient' is not altogether satisfactory either. It is true that the person to whom the communication comes may have a visual or auditory image, which slips into his mind apparently 'from nowhere' (that is, it has no connection with the thoughts or feelings which were occupying his mind a short time before). He may even have a visual or auditory hallucination, or a dream if he happens to be asleep at the time. But it is a little odd to call this 'perceiving'; '*re*ceiving' would be a better word. Probably it is now too late to alter these two terms 'agent' and 'percipient'. But we should notice that both of them are used in a very wide sense.

Moreover, it looks as if telepathy were a *two-stage* process, at any rate at the percipient's end. In the first stage, the 'impression' is received at some unconscious level of his mind; and then, in the second stage, it emerges in one way or another into his consciousness. Sometimes its emergence seems to be delayed until the percipient is asleep and it presents itself in the form of a dream. To speak metaphorically again, it is as if the telepathic impression, received at some unconscious level of the percipient's mind, were trying to emerge as best it can, and in order to do so, it probably has to overcome or circumvent some sort of biologically useful 'censorship'.

For if we are to succeed in our practical activities in this difficult and dangerous world—indeed if we are to remain alive—our physical environment must very often have the first claim on our attention. Too much telepathy, or at any rate too much of it at the conscious level, might well be disastrous. Imagine that someone has a vivid telepathic hallucination while he is trying to cross the High Street in the rush hour. Indeed, this applies to other paranormal experiences too. There is a story of a man who was in constant danger of being run over by taxicabs and other fast-moving vehicles when he walked in the streets of Paris; that was because he kept on having retrocognitive visions of the streets of *Roman* Paris. In some ways I envy this person. I should love to know what the streets of Paris looked like in the fourth century A.D. But this pleasure, great as it might be, would be rather a costly one.

A TELEPATHIC THEORY OF PETITIONARY PRAYER

Now let us consider a telepathic theory of petitionary prayer. It is a kind of extension of the agnostic's self-suggestion theory of prayer, which I have already discussed. We are all familiar with the distinction between three levels in the human mind: conscious, subconscious, and unconscious. At the conscious and subconscious levels, each of us is a separate individual. My thoughts and feelings are my own, and your thoughts and feelings are your own. I may try to tell you what my thoughts and feelings are, and you may try to tell me what yours are. But we cannot literally share them. Both of us may be afraid of the ferocious Alsatian dog across the street, and both of us may like the tabby cat which lives next door. But still, your fear of the dog and my fear of it are numerically different feelings, however similar they are, and the same applies to our respective likings for the cat.

Moreover, this is true at the subconscious level also, at least in one familiar sense of the word 'subconscious'—the sense in which there are mental events or mental states in each person's mind to which he is not in fact attending, though he could attend to them if he wished. To put it another way, there are mental states in all of us which are introspectible but not actually introspected. And two persons may differ very much in the amount of introspection that they do, in the degree of attention with which they do it, and also in the terminological resources which they have for describing (to themselves or to others) the introspective discoveries they have made: perhaps unpleasant or alarming ones, as when I notice myself feeling twinges of jealousy about the success or good fortune of some friend of mine.

But it is commonly supposed that there are mental events or mental states in each of us which are not introspectible at all and can only be revealed by indirect methods, such as dream analysis or the examination of seemingly accidental events (slips of the tongue, for instance, or forgetting someone's name though you know him quite well). We therefore postulate a third level in the human mind, the *unconscious* level.

UNCONSCIOUS PROBLEM-SOLVING

Nevertheless, we do not have to suppose (as a too-hasty reading of Freud might suggest) that the contents of the unconscious level are wholly disreputable, however disreputable some of them may be: unconscious hatred, for instance, or an unconscious 'death-wish' directed against another person. For this unconscious level of our minds is also the source of what is called 'creative thinking' or 'inspiration'; and these are rather grand names for something which occurs in some degree in all of us.

We all have problems of one sort or another, and very often we cannot solve them just by taking thought here and now. We have to wait until some possible solution 'occurs to us', as we say; and we probably find it helpful to expect (in a tranquil, not an anxious manner) that it will come to us if we wait for it. We may even suggest to ourselves that the solution of our problem will 'come to us' at a particular time, for instance after breakfast tomorrow morning when we start the day's work. Probably almost every writer uses this method when he 'gets stuck' in something he is trying to write.

The same applies to practical problems too, whether they are our own or those of someone else who has asked for our advice. We say to him, 'I can't give you the answer now. I must sleep on it. Come and ask me again tomorrow morning.' We are telling him, in effect, that he must allow time for our unconscious powers to work; we are also suggesting to ourselves that they will work, and quite often they do.

In such cases one is relying on unconscious mental processes in oneself, or at least that is what we usually believe. But if we now look again at the phenomena of telepathy, we begin to suspect that at the unconscious level there is no hard-and-fast distinction between one mind and another, however separate we may be at the conscious level. To put it in a frankly pictorial way, we begin to suspect that each of us is rather like a small peak emerging from a continuous mountain-range, or that we are like islands emerging from a continuous land-mass beneath the sea.

TELEPATHY AND THE COMMON UNCONSCIOUS

In the light of these rather speculative ideas, let us return to the problem of petitionary prayer. We can now propose a revised version of the self-suggestion theory of petitionary prayer. There were two difficulties in that theory. The first was that one may pray on behalf of other persons, and it seems that such prayers are answered sufficiently often to make this practice well worth while. The second difficulty was that even when a person prays on his own behalf, for deliverance from some trouble of his own, or for strength or guidance or intellectual enlightenment which he himself needs, his prayer is often answered through the actions of other people. Could we get over these difficulties by saying that the 'self', to which the suggestion is made, is not the individual self of you or me, but the Common Unconscious which somehow 'underlies' the individual minds of us all?

It might perhaps be objected that the Common Unconscious, as I have described it, does begin to look rather like the mind of God. In that case, the theory I have been stating is not at all what the *insipiens* wanted, but only a rather strange way of re-formulating the theistic theory of prayer which he rejects. But it is not very difficult to answer this objection. There is not the slightest reason to think that the Common Unconscious is omnipotent or omniscient. Moreover, God, according to theists, is wholly good. But we cannot ascribe any moral predicates at all to the Common Unconscious. So far as one can see, it is completely indifferent to the distinction between good and evil. Moreover, although it can quite properly be said to be the source of 'creative thinking', this is a metaphorical sense of the word 'creative'. What is called 'creative thinking' is not the production of something *ex nihilo*, as it would have to be if the word 'creative' were being used in its literal sense.

The old Aristotelian distinction between form and matter is relevant here. In a work of what we call 'original genius' the form is new, but the matter is old and familiar. Nothing quite like Shakespeare's *Othello* had ever been produced before. But the 'material' of it (if this phrase is permissible) consists of old and familiar human passions, love, hate, jealousy, and the like. Indeed, if it were not so, we could not understand the play when we read it or see it performed. The same is true of scientific originality, even when it amounts to original genius, as in Darwin's *Origin of Species* or the heliocentric theory of the relation between the earth, the sun, and the planets, whoever exactly it was who first invented it, whether it was Copernicus or one of the ancient Greek astronomers.

To use the terminology of John Locke: when some writer produces a new and original work, he has indeed produced some complex ideas which no one had thought of before. But still these complex ideas, however novel they are, can be analysed in terms of simpler ideas which are already familiar

to his readers. Otherwise his readers could not understand what
he has written, and he himself could not understand it either.

SOME DIFFICULTIES IN THIS THEORY OF PRAYER

Now let us return to the *insipiens*. He can quite properly find
some satisfaction in this non-theistic theory of 'how petitionary
prayer works'. Whatever view we take of the Common Unconscious, or of self-suggestion, or of telepathy, we have to
admit that there is nothing divine about any of them.

Nevertheless, there are some difficulties in this theory. They
are concerned with the concept of 'the Common Unconscious'
itself. If there is indeed a Common Unconscious, surely it
would follow that anyone you please could communicate
telepathically with anyone else you please, and on any topic
you please? And is there any reason to believe this?

Consider the thoughts which Einstein had when he was
constructing the Theory of Relativity. Could those thoughts
have been communicated telepathically to an Australian
bushman, or even to Einstein's charwoman in the next room?
It is possible that the emotional excitement of discovery might
have been communicated to them, or to the charwoman, at
any rate. This kind of excitement is something which has been
experienced at one time or another by everyone. Everyone
has problems, great or small, and knows what it feels like
when the solution begins to dawn on him. But surely the new
ideas which came into Einstein's mind at that time could only
have been communicated to someone who was already
familiar with the concepts and problems of Mathematical
Physics.

If so, it would follow that some of the limitations which
apply to ordinary verbal communication apply to telepathic
communication also. If Einstein had *spoken* to his charwoman
about the thoughts he was having at that time, he would still
have been unable to communicate them to her.

Again, it would be very surprising if a visual image could be
telepathically communicated to a person who had been blind

from birth; and if such a person experienced what is called a telepathic hallucination (the most dramatic of all forms of telepathic communication) it might be an auditory or tactual or olfactory hallucination, but it could not be a visual one. 'Visions' come only to persons who can see in the normal way, or at any rate to persons who have at one time been able to see in the normal way. The same applies to telepathic dreams.

It is, I think, convenient to go on using the phrase 'the Common Unconscious' when we are trying to understand the phenomena of telepathy. But we must not think of the Common Unconscious as if it were an undifferentiated mass of miscellaneous mental contents—yours and mine, Tom's, Dick's and Harry's, all lumped together. Not everything in it is common to everyone. The idea of pain is common to everyone. But the idea of red is not. Some people are colour-blind, and some are born totally blind and remain so all their lives. Might there also be emotions, reverence for example, which many people have experienced but some people have never experienced at all?

HOW DOES THE SUGGESTION GO TO THE RIGHT PERSON?

But whatever view we take about the Common Unconscious, there is another difficulty in the telepathic theory of petitionary prayer. This theory, as I have stated it, is a kind of extension of the familiar self-suggestion theory of prayer. But a critic might say that this explanation of 'how petitionary prayer works' is almost as puzzling as the theory of *ad hoc* divine interventions which claims that God 'answers' prayers by performing a minor miracle at our request.

As we have seen already, even when a person prays on his own behalf his prayer may well be 'answered' through the actions of someone else, perhaps someone quite unknown to him.[1] If we wish to explain this in terms of a 'telepathized'

[1] Cf. p. 44 above.

suggestion, how does it come about that the suggestion goes to the right person, the one who is able and willing to give me just the help or advice or information which I need? He may be someone I have never even heard of.

Am I issuing a kind of broadcast appeal—'This is what I need: please will anyone help me who can'? It seems to me that on the telepathic theory of prayer one is doing something of this kind when one prays on one's own behalf; and when one prays on another person's behalf, the broadcast appeal would be 'This is what So-and-so needs: please will anyone help him, or her, who can'? It is, I think, possible that telepathy might have this 'broadcast-like' character. Certainly it need not be directed to a particular other person though sometimes it is.

CONCLUSION

So much by way of a rough sketch of the telepathic theory of petitionary prayer. Does it give the *insipiens* what he wanted? I think that it does. But will it satisfy a religious person who knows by first-hand experience 'what it feels like' to pray? I am sure it will not, if his religion is of the theistic type, though if he is a Buddhist, conceivably it might. But a Christian, or indeed any theist, will object that this telepathic theory of petitionary prayer leaves something out: the personal relationship between man and God. He will insist that prayer is not just thinking, nor even wishing; it is *asking*. An 'I–thou' relation is an essential part of it. In petitionary prayer we are *addressing* one whom we love and trust, and we are sure that he loves us.

Is there any way of reconciling these two views of petitionary prayer, the psychical researcher's view and the theistic view? Or is a theist after all compelled to maintain that whenever our prayers are answered God works a minor miracle at our request? That would be a very unwelcome conclusion for the theist himself, even perhaps a self-contradictory one; for, as I have suggested already, if miracles were always happening, hundreds or even thousands of them every day, there would no longer be any meaning in calling them 'miracles'.

But I think the theist has another alternative. He might say, instead, that when and if we sincerely place ourselves in this 'I–thou' relationship with God, and make our requests to him, the very fact that we do so 'releases' paranormal forces of some kind, and these in their turn bring about the result which we asked for. If so, there is after all nothing *ad hoc* or miraculous about the way our prayers are answered. Instead, the request itself, if we make it in the appropriate 'I–thou' manner, brings about the conditions which are necessary for its fulfilment.

4

LATENT SPIRITUAL CAPACITIES

I USE the word 'latent' in the sense given in the *Shorter Oxford English Dictionary*. By 'a latent capacity' I mean one which is 'hidden or concealed; existing, but not developed or manifested'. For instance, a child brought up in the wilds of Borneo might have a capacity for higher mathematics. But this capacity might remain undeveloped, unused, all his life, and neither he nor anyone else would be aware that he had it.

What do I mean by the word 'spiritual'? A difficult question indeed! I will only say for the moment that I wish to distinguish between spiritual capacities on the one hand and paranormal capacities on the other. The capacities I wish to discuss are those which are manifested in religious experience (first-hand religious experience), especially in the religious experiences which are characteristic of the higher religions; and the hypothesis I wish to discuss is that every normal human being is capable of having such first-hand religious experiences, whether he knows it or not.

But even if everyone has these capacities, there are many who do not use them, and do not even suspect that they possess them, particularly in this present epoch. In our present technological Western civilization—one of the most *un*spiritual, perhaps, in all human history—these capacities often remain latent or undeveloped.

There may also be latent capacities of the paranormal kind, capacities for telepathy, clairvoyance, precognition, and perhaps others (for instance, a capacity for telekinesis). It may well be that such capacities are not confined to a small group of 'psychically gifted' people; they may be present in a latent form in many other persons, perhaps in everyone.

What is the relation between paranormal capacities and spiritual capacities? That is a very puzzling question too. If we take extreme cases on either side, it may seem that these two realms, the paranormal and the spiritual, are completely different and have no connection at all with one another. For instance, successful card-guessing (as in the well-known experiments of Dr. Rhine and Dr. Soal)[1] is something very different indeed from a mystical experience of 'union with God'.

Perhaps we may put it this way: telepathy, clairvoyance, precognition, and retrocognition are short-cuts, as it were, by which people become aware of facts which can also be found out by normal methods, just by using our normal capacities of sense-perception, introspection, and memory; and these normal methods are the ones we use for *testing* or verifying the information given to us by those who claim to have 'psychic' gifts. That is what we do, for instance, when someone claims to have had a telepathic or precognitive dream about a railway accident, or claims to have discovered the contents of a sealed letter by means of clairvoyance. Does this paranormally acquired information correspond with facts which can be established by normal observation, and is the correspondence so close and detailed that it cannot reasonably be explained by chance coincidence? Or again, does it correspond in a similarly detailed manner with facts which can be established by introspection, as when a psychically gifted person tells me about thoughts or wishes or feelings of my own which I have never mentioned to anyone?

We use a similar procedure when we try to decide whether mediumistic communications are veridical. Does the alleged communicator mention any facts—facts about *this* world—which we can verify by means of observation or memory or biographical research? If he does, this gives some support to the hypothesis that he is the deceased person he claims to be. It is evidence, at any rate, that something of a paranormal kind is happening.

[1] See, e.g., J. B. Rhine, *New World of the Mind* (London, 1954).

But spiritual experiences do not seem to be 'short-cuts' of this kind. They put some people in touch with a level of reality which is not accessible in any other way, or at least it is claimed that they do. Consequently, what we are told by such people cannot be tested or verified by using our normal cognitive powers of sense-perception, introspection, and memory. The only way of testing or verifying what they tell us would be to have similar experiences for ourselves, at first hand; and if we have never had any, the best we can do is to follow the scriptural injunction 'By their fruits ye shall know them'. The fruits we have to look for are described by St. Paul when he says 'the fruit of the Spirit is love, joy, peace'.

So far, it may seem that there is a clear distinction of kind between the paranormal and the spiritual. It is, however, true that saintly people, in all the higher religions, sometimes have paranormal gifts as well. They seem to have acquired these paranormal powers in their stride, as it were, as a by-product of the stage of spiritual development which they have reached.

It is also true that there are experiences of a visionary kind —Swedenborg's visions of 'higher worlds', for example—and these experiences seem to be intermediate between the psychical and the spiritual or a kind of mixture of the two. Here again we have no way of testing the information which is offered to us, unless or until we can manage to have similar experiences ourselves. We are in similar difficulties with mediumistic communications or automatic writings which claim to describe 'other' worlds and what goes on in them. Ordinary observation does not help us here, if we wish to test or verify the information which is offered to us. Historical research may tell us that other people in other ages have had rather similar experiences. But that does not help us to decide whether such experiences have any objective basis. Moreover, if they have—if they throw any light at all on 'what there is' outside ourselves—one suspects that the level of reality which they reveal is one in which our ordinary common-sense distinction between the symbolic and the literal does not apply.

Perhaps the wisest course is just to suspend judgement on these questions for the present, and to put such narratives away in a pigeon-hole at the back of our minds in case they should ever become useful later. A senior colleague of mine in the Society for Psychical Research once told me that this was what he did himself, and advised me to do likewise. I think it was good advice.

But a point which is more relevant to my present argument is this: even if we think that such visionary experiences do reveal aspects or levels of reality which the normal person cannot reach, we must admit that they are still experiences of 'the world of Name and Form', to use the Hindu terminology, and not of the Infinite Being who is beyond Name and Form. Or as a Christian theist would put it, these experiences of 'other worlds' (extraordinary though they are) are still concerned with *created* things and not with the Creator, even though these created things are very different from those which we observe by means of the senses. If there are indeed heavens and hells, purgatories and paradises, they are still part of the created universe, however wonderful or however terrifying they may be.

If I am right so far, we do have to draw a distinction between psychical or paranormal capacities on the one hand, and spiritual capacities on the other, even though there are persons in whom both sorts of capacity have been aroused from the latent or dormant state which they have in the ordinary man; and even though there may be experiences which are both spiritual and psychical at the same time, for example some of those described in the Book of Revelation, or the vision described in the Book of Isaiah, ch. 6.

SPIRITUAL CAPACITIES

May I now remind you that I mean by 'spiritual capacities' the ones which are used in first-hand religious experiences, and the hypothesis I wish to discuss is that capacities of this kind exist in every human being. But even if we do think that everyone has them, we have to admit that there are many who do not use them and in whom they remain latent or undeveloped.

It is indeed possible that these capacities are not wholly dormant even in someone who does not consciously use them and has never even suspected that he has them. They might still operate in him in some degree at an unconscious or a subconscious level. Much may go on in our minds which we are not conscious of at all. And much may also go on 'at the back of our minds', as we say (at the margin of the field of attention, to put it more technically). Obscure and rather disturbing 'intimations' or 'inklings' may come to us some-times, and we are half-aware of them when they come, but we do not attend to them, and forget them almost immediately afterwards.

Again, many people feel a certain dissatisfaction sometimes with the world as it is revealed by means of sense-organs, the familiar physical and social environment in which they live, and have the thought that some better or more satisfying kind of experience is possible. The feeling of not being alto-gether at home in this world, the idea that our highest good is not to be found there, probably comes to many people occasionally; and perhaps it comes to them because their spiritual capacities are not wholly dormant, but are operating in some degree at an unconscious or subconscious level. Usually this feeling of dissatisfaction passes away after a while. But if it is strong and persistent, it may be the starting-point of what is called 'the religious quest' in one of the many forms which that quest may take.

Some thinkers have even argued that because the world of normal experience is unsatisfying, there *must* be something better. It seems to me that this is a bad argument, though in one form or another it has quite often been used. We cannot get conclusions about matters of fact, conclusions about 'what there is' (for example 'there is a God', 'there are other worlds', 'there is a life after death') from premises of a purely evalu-ative kind. The argument I have been suggesting is quite different, and I think more plausible. If we do have spiritual capacities and if they can operate unconsciously, we might expect that they would manifest themselves by feelings of dissatisfaction with the world of normal everyday experience; and such feelings do in fact occur in many human beings from time to time.

THE VILLAGE OF ERITH

So far I have only been telling you what I mean by this rather mysterious phrase 'latent spiritual capacities'. Now the hypothesis that we all have these capacities, at least in a latent form, is relevant to a well-known criticism of religion, a criticism which was first formulated by the Logical Positivist philosophers in the 1920s and still has great influence. We are told that such statements as 'God exists' or 'There is a God who loves us' are empty or devoid of meaning. They look as if they were statements of fact. But surely they cannot be, because there is no conceivable way of testing them or verifying them: and so the only function they can have is to express what one might call cosmic emotions. For instance if a man says 'God orders all things for the best', we shall be told that he is not making a statement which is true or even false. What he is trying to say is something like 'Hurrah for the universe!'. But he has said it in a misleading or muddled way, as if he were making a statement of fact.

Some of you may have come across a little poem about the village of Erith (I believe there is such a place). It has always given me great pleasure, and we may use it as a kind of parable to illustrate this criticism of religious statements. It goes like this:

> There are men in the village of Erith
> Whom nobody seeth or heareth;
> And there looms on the marge
> Of the river a barge
> Which nobody roweth or steereth.

We will not trouble about the barge, though a religious significance could be given to this too, and also to the river. (There is an Eastern idea, found both in Hinduism and in Buddhism, that a religion is like a boat which takes us safely across the sea of *Samsara*, the flux of phenomenal events.) But we will only consider the men whom nobody seeth or heareth. We will suppose that no one touches them either, and that they leave no observable traces of themselves such as footprints or fingerprints. Nor does anyone in the village find that a piece of cheese is missing from the larder, or that a bottle of wine has mysteriously disappeared from the cellar. There is absolutely no perceptual evidence for the existence of these men. On the other hand, there is no way of being certain that they do not exist. If they were not there, everything that goes on in the village of Erith would be just the same as it is now. But equally, if they *were* there, everything which goes on in the village would be just the same as it is now.

So if we assert that such men exist in the village of Erith, surely our assertion is completely empty? We have described those men in such a way that there is no conceivable way of settling the question 'Do they exist or not?'. This question, therefore (we shall be told), is itself empty or devoid of meaning. For surely a question is not intelligible—it is not a genuine question at all—unless there is some conceivable way of settling it? There might indeed be no practicable way of settling the question 'Are there mountains on the other side of the moon?' (an example used by the Logical Positivist philosophers themselves). But it was always conceivable that the question might be settled some day by means of observational evidence, direct or indirect. And we now have photographic evidence which supports the answer 'Yes'.

The application of our parable about the village of Erith is now fairly obvious. The village of Erith is the observable universe, and the men whom nobody seeth or heareth are the gods of all the various religions—and also any other supernatural beings which religious persons claim to tell us about, for example angels or demons. The argument of these philosophers, if it be valid, disposes of all the religions, poly-theistic or monotheistic, with the possible exception of Pan-theism,[1] in which the observable universe itself is the only object of worship. With that possible exception, all the religions make supernatural claims of one kind or another.

The fundamental point in this criticism of religion is that statements about God are unverifiable, or that there is no conceivable way of testing them. This is because God is by definition a transcendent or supernatural being. He cannot be found anywhere in the observable universe.

Perhaps it will be said that there have been times when he *was* found there, and that we have empirical evidence of this in the form of historical testimony. It is of course claimed in some religious traditions that God has been incarnated in this world at least once, or even many times according to the Hindu religious tradition (Christianity is not the only 'incar-nationist' religion). But the philosophers I have in mind will not be greatly troubled by such claims. Their reply to them would be something like this: even if we do think that God has been incarnated in this observable world at least once, we still have to admit that his divine attributes were not dis-coverable by means of the senses, though his human attributes were. To discern his divine attributes, the 'eye of faith' was needed. To those who did not have it, he was just a very extraordinary human being, a man of genius perhaps, pos-sessed of very remarkable paranormal powers, a supremely great ethical teacher, but still a human being and no more. The same 'eye of faith' is needed by us now when we read the Gospels. Otherwise we shall see no more in him than his own unbelieving contemporaries did, though we may admire him greatly, as no doubt some of them did. What is this 'eye of faith'? According to the philosophers we are discussing, it is no more than a muddled way of speaking and thinking. They

---

[1] I call it 'a possible exception', because there are perhaps forms of Pan-theism (held by some of the so-called 'Nature Mystics') in which the universe is supposed to have properties other than, or additional to, those which can be observed by means of the senses.

will tell us that no intelligible sense can be given to the adjective 'divine'; so we do not know what we mean when we say that a particular historical person was divine as well as human.

INSIDERS AND OUTSIDERS

So much for the Positivistic criticisms of religion. They have had, and still have, great influence, perhaps because they state in a clear and forceful way a kind of uneasiness which has been at the back of many people's minds for a very long time. Many a man would say that the statements of religious people 'mean nothing to him' or that he 'cannot make any sense of them'. What is the good of setting out on the religious quest, as it is called, if the only result you can expect from it is a habit of talking nonsense to yourself and to others?

It is true that no one who is already religious would be much moved by the arguments of these Positivist philosophers. He would reply that it is they, and not he, who do not know what they are talking about, because they are speaking about religion from the outside, without any personal experience of what it is actually like to be religious. I think this is a fair reply as far as it goes. There is a distinction here between insiders and outsiders. Newman makes a remark about religious devotion which is worth quoting. 'We meet with men of the world', he says, 'who cannot enter into the very idea of devotion . . . because they know of no exercise of the affections beyond what is merely human.'[1] We meet with such persons among the learned too. There are psychologists, sociologists, and philosophers who cannot enter into the idea of devotion either, because they have no personal experience of what it is like to be in that condition.

But this is not a very satisfactory reply to the criticisms we are considering. It has too much of a *tu quoque* character. If I am accused of talking nonsense, I do not dispose of the charge by saying 'you do not know what you are talking

[1] *Grammar of Assent* (Longmans, 1947), ch. iii, p. 24.

about either'. It is still conceivable that neither of us knows what he is talking about, and that there are muddles or misconceptions of one sort or another on both sides.

What a defender of religion must try to do, if it can be done, is to meet these philosophical critics on their own ground. He must try to show that religious statements *are* testable or verifiable after all; or at least, that evidence can be found which supports them, even though we cannot get conclusive evidence for them in this present life.

Will the hypothesis of latent spiritual capacities help us to do this? Perhaps it will. You notice that it is not a hypothesis about God or about any supernatural entity. It is a hypothesis about ourselves, about human nature or human personality.

'SEEK AND YE SHALL FIND'

Now let me remind you of two well-known sayings which are attributed to Jesus in the New Testament: 'Seek and ye shall find', 'Knock and it shall be opened unto you'. There is a certain difference of emphasis between them, and I shall have something to say about that later. But for the present let us just consider 'Seek and ye shall find'. I think that something analogous to it might be found in other religious traditions also. At any rate, the idea of a 'religious quest' of some kind, and the belief that it is possible to succeed in it, is found in all the higher religions.

From a logical point of view 'Seek and ye shall find' resembles 'Ask and ye shall receive', which was discussed in the chapter on petitionary prayer.[1] We might paraphrase it thus: 'If you seek, you will find: therefore seek.' It is a combination of a conditional proposition on the one hand and a command or invitation on the other. The command or invitation is neither true nor false. It cannot be verified, or falsified either. All we can do about it is to act on it or refrain from acting on it. The conditional proposition, on the

---

[1] Above, pp. 40–1.

F

other hand, *is* either true or false. It can be verified or falsified. We can test it by acting in the way recommended.

There is another resemblance between 'Seek and ye shall find' and 'Ask and ye shall receive'. It is *not* said that asking is a necessary condition for receiving, but only that it is a sufficient condition. If asking were a necessary condition for receiving, the appropriate formulation would be 'You will not receive unless you ask' or 'You will receive only if you ask'. The same applies to 'Seek and ye shall find'. If seeking were a necessary (indispensable) condition for finding, one would have to say 'You will not find unless you seek'; and this, according to the testimony of religious people, would be false. They would tell us that men do sometimes find God without seeking him. Or perhaps we should say that God finds them; he meets them or encounters them though they were not looking for him. What 'Seek and ye shall find' conveys is that seeking God is a *sufficient* condition for finding him. One might still have to seek for a very long time, and it might be a very difficult process. How long it takes, and how difficult it is, might depend upon the kind of person you are. One person might have more hindrances to overcome than another, though everyone has some. But what this conditional prediction says is that if we sincerely seek for God, we can be sure of finding him in the end. And it is claimed that the prediction applies to everyone, no matter who he is.

The most important point for our argument is that 'Seek and ye shall find' is a saying which can be tested. We test it by actually seeking. There is, no doubt, something peculiar about this seeking. The 'place' or 'region' in which we are invited to seek is not the outer world perceived by means of the senses. It would be useless to seek for God by means of a telescope or by means of space travel. The seeking, and the finding too if it happens, takes place primarily in our own inner life. Outward things and happenings may indeed be relevant to it. For instance, meeting and talking to another person, or reading what he has written, may be highly relevant; but only because of the influence it has on our own inner life. We must ourselves attend to what he tells us, be interested and moved by it, and try to make it our own. Consequently, if we are so behaviouristic that we think there is no inner life in anyone, not even in ourselves, or that it makes no sense to say there is, the process of seeking for God cannot even begin. A behaviouristic theory so extreme as this would cut off religion at the very roots. But I do not see how anyone can sincerely apply such a theory to himself, however determined he is to apply it to his neighbours. I will be bold enough to say that everyone *knows* that he himself has an inner life, however little interest he may take in what goes on in it.

We can now see that 'Seek and ye shall find' is closely connected with the hypothesis of latent spiritual capacities. If you seek for God, you will find him, no matter who you are. This implies that everyone has the capacity for seeking for God, whether he knows it or not. It may hitherto have been latent—unused, unactualized—but he can use it if he wishes. The Gospel saying also implies that we all have the capacity for finding God, whether we know it or not. Everyone has it, though it is latent or dormant in many of us. The process of seeking will awaken it or arouse it from its dormant state. It might be that there are degrees of 'finding'. But everyone, if he sincerely and persistently seeks, will find in some degree.

It may be noticed, on the other hand, that no one is compelled to seek. We may seek or not, as we choose. The same applies to the other saying 'Knock and it shall be opened unto you'. It is our choice to knock or not. It may be that there is in all of us a kind of wish or need to seek for God, even if we are not ourselves aware of this wish or need. Perhaps this is the point of Pascal's paradox 'Thou couldst not seek me unless thou hadst already found me', and of St. Augustine's remark 'Thou hast made us for thyself and our heart is unquiet until it rests in thee'. Nevertheless, there may also be in all of us a wish of just the opposite kind: a wish to keep away from God and have nothing to do with him, to be 'on our own' in a state of sovereign independence. Still, if we have these two opposed wishes, it is in our power to choose between them.

The conflict between these wishes, and the possibility of choosing between them, is illustrated in the parable of the Prodigal Son. The life of the man who tries to live without God is represented there as a kind of exile, and moreover a voluntary exile, which is ended by an equally voluntary return. One way of realizing how much you need something is to deprive yourself of it and try to do without it. But according to the parable you do not have to remain in exile. You can go home again if you choose, however long and difficult the journey may be; and you will receive a warm welcome when you get there.

ONE WAY OF 'SEEKING'

So far, it seems that seeking for God is not something we are compelled to do. We do it by our own choice. But how do we set about it? I suspect that there are several different answers to this question. It may even be that every person seeks in his own way and finds in his own way too, if he does find. In theistic religion at any rate, in which the concept of love is central (God's love for us and our love for him), we might expect that each person would seek, and find, in his own way, since everyone loves in his own way. If love is something like giving oneself to another, each one of us has a different self to give. And even though procedures which are roughly similar may be used by many persons, we shall not be surprised if there are differences between one person's way of seeking and another's. Each one of us is a unique individual, and his religion, if he has any, is perhaps the most personal thing about him.

So I shall just discuss *one* way of seeking for God. The starting-point of it is the impression which is made upon us by certain sorts of testimony, the testimony of persons who are themselves already religious. It might be either spoken or written testimony, or a combination of both.

There are some people to whom first-hand religious experience comes spontaneously, without any conscious effort on their part. Even mystical experiences come to some people in this spontaneous way. There are some who find without seeking. But such persons are very rare, especially in this age. Most of us nowadays have to begin by accepting the testimony of other seekers, who have already gone some way along the road and claim that it is leading them somewhere. Or rather, we begin not quite by accepting their testimony, but by taking it seriously because we are impressed by the kind of characters which they have. 'The fruit of the spirit is love, joy, peace.' This fruit, when we meet with it in some person whom we know, impresses us and attracts us for its own sake, even though we have only the dimmest conception of what it is the fruit of. The very best advertisement for any religious teaching is the charity, compassion, and inward serenity of those who practise it. And so we are disposed to listen to the testimony such people give us. They tell us that there is a God, that he loves every one of us, and that our own highest good consists in loving him. Strange words! We do not know what to make of them, and so far as we can make any sense of them, they sound too good to be true. Indeed, from the point of view of the 'natural man', whose attention is wholly concentrated on his physical and social environment, they *are* too good to be true. But need one remain for ever in the position of the natural man? Might one get out of it? Perhaps it might be worth while to try.

This is the first step, taking the testimony of religious people seriously, thinking that there might conceivably be 'something in it', and that it is worth while trying to find out whether there is.

But now we come to a difficulty, connected with the distinction between 'insiders' and 'outsiders' which was mentioned earlier. For instance, we may be told by our religious friends to pray to God (to ask for his forgiveness or his help). But how can we possibly pray to him unless we already believe that he exists? More difficult still, we may be told to try to love him. But how can we possibly try to love him unless we already believe that he exists and moreover that he is lovable?

May I remind you again of the words of Pascal? 'Thou couldst not seek me unless thou hadst already found me.' Certainly we can make some sense of this if we are already within the religious attitude. Then we shall say that the impulse to seek for God is itself the effect of God's grace, so that the seeker is already in touch with God at an unconscious or subconscious level, and in that sense has already found him. Or we might put it the other way round: we can only seek for God if he has already found us. (Compare the parable of the Good Shepherd who seeks and finds the lost sheep.) But these things *can* only be said from within the religious attitude: and the question is, how can a person ever get inside this attitude unless he is in some way inside it already?

'NOT FAR FROM EVERY ONE OF US'

Perhaps we can get some light on this difficulty, if we consider something else which our religious friends may have told us. They may have told us (they probably did) that this mysterious being whom they speak of is *accessible* to all of us— 'not far from every one of us', as St. Paul put it in his sermon to the Athenians.[1] And not only that: they probably told us also what kind of accessibility he has, or in what sense he is 'accessible'. According to their testimony, he is accessible in the sense that we can enter into personal relations with him, and even in the sense that he invites us to enter into such personal relations with him. I have already mentioned 'Knock and it shall be opened unto you'. But there is another scriptural image in which the situation is reversed. 'Behold, *I* stand at the door and knock.' He himself asks us to open our door and let him in. If one may say it with reverence, he asks us to treat him as a friend.

The important point here is that the God of theism is not merely 'He' but 'Thou'. And this, I think, is what theists

[1] Acts 17: 27.

mean by describing him as 'personal'. He is not merely one who can be spoken *about*: he can be spoken *to* or addressed. Moreover, they tell us that if we try to address him, as humbly and respectfully as we can, he will respond and welcome us. It is hard to believe this, or even to understand it clearly, but how can we be sure that it is false (or unintelligible) until we do try?

It follows from this that seeking for God is not at all like seeking for an inanimate object, a mountain perhaps in some unexplored part of the earth. Seeking for God is more like trying to *meet* someone whom you have heard of and have never yet met: someone moreover (so you are told) who wants to meet you and will welcome you when you find him.

From this again it follows that the heart, as well as the head, enters into the search for God. Of course this is very awkward. The seeking is not just an attempt to settle an important theoretical question. We shall never manage to find the one whom we seek unless we are willing to love him when found. Dare I say, we must *want* him?[1] The finding, if we do find, will consist in 'loving him who first loved us'. The words of St. John 'we love him, because he first loved us' are the classical formulation of the theistic type of religious experience.[2]

If one were to seek for God with the head only, at the best one would only find 'the God of the philosophers and the men of science', *le dieu des philosophes et des savans*, and not 'the God of Abraham, Isaac and Jacob'. That is how Pascal put it.

'The God of the philosophers and the men of science' is the God whom those learned persons used to have in Pascal's own time, the seventeenth century. This God is not 'Thou' but only 'He', or perhaps only 'it'—the Supreme Being, the First Cause, or the Absolute. A man might be convinced on theoretical grounds that such a Supreme Entity exists without being a religious person in the least. 'The God of Abraham, Isaac and Jacob', on the other hand, is 'Thou' as well as 'He', one whom we can speak to and one with whom we can

---

[1] Cf. Psalm 42: 1: 'Like as the hart desireth the waterbrooks . . .'
[2] 1 John 4: 19.

have personal relations of love, reverence, obedience, and trust.

SEEKING AND ADDRESSING

If we seek for him, then, we must do it by trying to address him. The agnostic's prayer 'O God, if there be a God, save my soul, if I have a soul' was not wholly absurd. He did at least use the vocative case, and what he said was at least a prayer, though a very odd one.

But still, how can we address someone unless we already believe that he exists? Once again, we encounter the difficulty about 'insiders' and 'outsiders', the difficulty (or rather, the paradox) that apparently we cannot become religious unless we are religious already. There must surely be some solution of it, since people do in fact manage to become religious who were not at all religious before. If we conceive of the seeking as an attempt to enter into a personal relationship with God, and of the finding as the establishment of such a personal relationship, perhaps the difficulty becomes a little less troublesome.

For surely we can at least *try* to address someone, even though we are not sure that he exists. A man who has fallen into a river in the dark can shout 'Help! Help!' The situation of the 'natural man', who has as yet had no first-hand religious experience, does sometimes resemble that of a man who has fallen into a river in the dark. That is something which could be expected to happen sooner or later to many of the inhabitants of the village of Erith. And perhaps someone whom nobody seeth or heareth at other times *can* be heard in such circumstances. Perhaps you can only hear him if you try to speak to him first. Or perhaps we could have heard him in other circumstances too, if only we had listened more carefully. Those who claim to know him tell us that he sometimes speaks in 'a still, small voice'.

It is unfortunate that we have to discuss these important matters in pictorial language, by the use of metaphors and analogies, and perhaps I should apologize for talking so much about the village of Erith. The difficulty is that first-hand religious experience is something different from any other experience which we have. I think that addressing another human being and hearing his reply is about the best analogy which we can find; but it is only an analogy. The response which we receive, if we do receive one, is not literally heard with the outward ears. It comes to us inwardly, if it does come. And the same is true of addressing, the attempt to speak to someone about whom our religious friends have told us. This too is inward, even though the words may be spoken aloud. At any rate, it is the inward attitude expressed by them which matters, and there may quite well be no outward words at all.

But since analogies do have to be used, let me offer another. Suppose I am told that there is someone who likes me very much and wishes to meet me, though I have never met him. I am also told that he is very near me all the time, though I never noticed him because it is so very dark hereabouts, or perhaps the trouble is that I am half-blind. (This is the sort of thing I *am* told by my religious friends.) I do not believe what I am told. It seems very unlikely to be true. All the same, I cannot help being a little moved by this extraordinary story, the more so because I cannot help respecting those who tell it. So I think it worth while to try to speak to this person whom they tell me about, and say 'Thank you very much for taking this friendly interest in me' just on the chance that he may be there. And it seems to me that I get a kind response, though it is difficult to hear. So I try again later—perhaps I try many times—and by degrees it comes to seem to me that I hear his replies a little more clearly.

ACTING 'AS IF' WITHOUT BELIEVING

What I have done here is to act as if a hypothesis were true. I did not have to begin by accepting the hypothesis, though I did have to begin by taking an interest in it, and by being prepared to take a certain amount of trouble in order to find out whether or not it is true. Perhaps we cannot hope to get conclusive evidence either way (evidence which will settle the question completely) but we do hope to get evidence which will be relevant to it. So we act as if the hypothesis were true in order to test it. We follow the procedures recommended by our religious friends, not because we are already sure that these procedures will work (we are not yet sure of this at all) but in order to discover whether they do work—whether they do in fact have the results which we are told that they have.

Perhaps we can now see how the paradox about 'insiders' and 'outsiders' can be solved. The paradox was that apparently one can never get 'inside' the religious attitude unless one is inside it already. For example, in order to get inside it you are told to *address* God (to pray to him, or to express penitence to him, or to thank him). But how can you address someone unless you already believe that he exists and is in some degree accessible to you?

The paradox is solved when we distinguish between believing a hypothesis and acting (inwardly) as if it were true. It is easy to confuse the two, because a man who believes the hypothesis does also act as if it were true. For example, the man who believes that God exists and is accessible will certainly address him. Nevertheless, a man who does not believe, or not yet, can act as if a hypothesis were true, in order to test it and find out whether it can or cannot be verified. And that is what the seeker for God has to do.

This, then, is one way of interpreting the sentence in the Gospel 'Seek and ye shall find'. According to this interpretation, it is a conditional prediction: 'If you seek for God, you will find him.' And it is claimed that this prediction can be tested or verified by acting as if it were true. I would emphasize again that the action required is an inward one. This is still true, even though it is an action of trying to address someone or speak to someone. Certainly this inward action may also express itself in outward behaviour. The seeker may go to church and join in the service, saying the prayers aloud or singing the hymns. But it is possible to do all these things in a purely external way, without attending to the meaning of what we say or sing. What matters is the inward attitude with which we do them. We must put our hearts and minds into the words which we utter. And it is not necessary that we should utter any outward words at all.

Moreover, the response which we eventually receive (if there is one) is also received inwardly. We cannot prove to someone else that we have indeed received it. If he says, as he very likely will, 'It is all a purely imaginative exercise', there is no way of convincing him. Or perhaps he will say, 'We all know already that the *idea* of God has great psychological power, and is liable to produce strong emotions in someone who pays a good deal of attention to it.' Again, we have no way of convincing him that we have experienced anything more than strong emotions. I am afraid that religion *is* a private and personal matter. How can it be anything else, if it consists (as theists say it does) in having a personal relationship with God? All we can say to the outsider is 'Try it and see for yourself'.

PELAGIUS

There is, however, an objection which may fairly be made form *inside* the religious attitude. It may be objected that my interpretation of 'Seek and ye shall find' is altogether too Pelagian. Pelagius lived in the latter part of the fourth century and the early part of the fifth. It seems that he came from this country, and may therefore be regarded as the first British philosopher. Pelagius is supposed to have held that we can 'save ourselves' by our own voluntary efforts.[1] He was criticized for this by one of the greatest of all Christian thinkers,

---

[1] May I say that I have a considerable admiration for him? Making an important philosophical mistake is no small service to mankind.

his contemporary St. Augustine, and his views were con-
demned as heretical.

You may well think that I too have represented the seeking
for God as a purely 'do it yourself' affair, and have said little
or nothing about the grace of God. Surely the seeking is itself
the effect of God's grace? (He was 'drawing us to himself'
though we did not know it.) If we persist in seeking, in spite
of difficulties and disappointments, surely that is the effect of
God's grace too? And if in the end we have the experience of
finding him, in some degree at any rate, what really happens
is that he discloses himself to us. Or, if you like to put it so,
we do not find him but he finds us. All we have to do ourselves
is to accept God's grace, or refrain from resisting it.

'KNOCK AND IT SHALL BE OPENED UNTO YOU'

There is much force in these objections. I admit that I have
presented a somewhat one-sided picture in what I have said
about seeking and finding. This one-sidedness can perhaps be
corrected if we remember the context in which the sentence
'Seek and ye shall find' occurs. In the Gospel passage from
which I quoted there are three sentences of the same logical
form, 'Do such-and-such, and such-and-such results will follow'.
'Ask and ye shall receive. Seek and ye shall find. Knock and
it shall be opened unto you.' All three may be interpreted as
conditional predictions.

I shall not say anything now about the first sentence, 'Ask
and ye shall receive'. I have already said more than enough
about it in the chapter on petitionary prayer, though every
religious person would claim that it is verifiable, provided
that we ask in a humble, trusting, and loving frame of mind.
But I should like to draw your attention to the last sentence
of the three, 'Knock and it shall be opened unto you'.

To correct the one-sided 'do it yourself' impression which I
may have given, the two sentences 'Seek and ye shall find',
'Knock and it shall be opened unto you' should be taken
together. At first, it may seem that they are two ways of saying

the same thing. But there is at least an important difference of emphasis between them. Both seeking and finding are things which *we* do. But in 'Knock and it shall be opened unto you' there is only one thing which we do. All we have to do is to knock on the door. But the opening of the door is not something which we do. It is done for us by someone else.

This has a bearing on the concept of a latent spiritual capacity, and on the hypothesis that we all possess such capacities, at any rate in a latent form. Perhaps we should think of them not, or not only, as capacities for doing something—seeking for God—but also as capacities for receiving something, or being acted upon by something outside ourselves. If we do have spiritual capacities, a capacity for receiving God's grace must certainly be one of them. There is a parallel for this in the more familiar sphere of sense-perception. We have a capacity for discerning objects in our physical environment by means of sight and hearing. But we could not make any use of it unless we were capable of being acted upon by the appropriate sorts of physical stimuli (light-rays and sound-waves). In a similar way, perhaps, we need to have a capacity for being affected by God's grace, in order to seek for him and find him.

But even though his grace does come to us—to every one of us, perhaps, whether we recognize it or not—it is still in our power to resist it, and we frequently do. God does not compel anyone to love him. Love has to be given freely. It cannot be compelled.

To speak now in frankly religious language, God himself asks for the love of free and autonomous personal beings, who freely accept his love for them and freely give him their love in return. That, I think, is what is conveyed in the words 'Behold, *I* stand at the door and knock'.

5

MOTIVES FOR DISBELIEF IN LIFE AFTER DEATH

In Book XI of the *Odyssey* Odysseus visits the Next World, and has a conversation with Achilles, who 'holds mighty sway' among the dead. It turns out, however, that Achilles is very far from being content with this exalted situation. This is what he says:

> Βουλοίμην κ' ἐπάρουρος ἐὼν θητευέμεν ἄλλῳ,
> ἀνδρὶ παρ' ἀκλήρῳ, ᾧ μὴ βίοτος πολὺς εἴη,
> ἢ πᾶσιν νεκύεσσι καταφθιμένοισιν ἀνάσσειν.

'I would rather be a serf tied to the soil, serving a man with few possessions and a poor livelihood, than reign as king over all the departed dead.'

I have quoted these splendid lines in order to suggest that the belief in life after death is not necessarily a comforting one at all. Achilles, you notice, was not in some Hell or Purgatory. He had the best position which anyone in the Next World could have, at any rate in Homer's opinion. These words of Achilles are relevant to the very widespread view that belief in life after death is no more than 'wishful thinking'—believing a proposition to be true merely because we wish it to be true.

It is indeed obvious that the question whether human personality continues to exist after death cannot be settled by considering our wishes. It is a complicated question: partly a question of fact, but partly also a conceptual or philosophical question concerning the concept of 'a person'. For example, does it make sense to speak of 'a disembodied person'? Or again, suppose that after Mr. A's death there is an entity which remembers Mr. A's experiences in this life and accepts them as having been its own, but no longer has the capacity for thinking new thoughts or making voluntary decisions. We might then want to say a part of Mr. A's personality continued to exist after death, but not the whole of it.

Thus the question divides into two: a factual question on the one hand, and a theoretical or conceptual question on the other. But our wishes are entirely irrelevant to both these questions. On the face of it, at any rate, however much people wish to survive death, this has no relevance whatever to the question whether they will in fact survive it. There are also those who wish *not* to survive death—one life is quite enough for them—but it is still perfectly possible that they will in fact survive whether they like it or not. Again, there may be some who wish *not* to survive death themselves, but wish that other people may survive it; I suspect that there are a good many persons, especially in our present too strenuous society, who have this combination of wishes. But of all the possible alternatives, this is perhaps the one which is least likely to be fulfilled.

It would seem, then, that in discussing the problem of life after death we should put our wishes entirely out of our minds, just as we should in discussing a question of geology or astronomy. But we all know that this is a very difficult thing to do. There are indeed some people who say they are emotionally indifferent to the question whether they will survive death or not. What matters, they tell us, is the quality of one's life, not its duration. 'One day in Thy courts is better than a thousand.' We can all sympathize with such people; more than that, we can and should congratulate them. This kind of emotional indifference is something wholly admirable.

But there is another kind of indifference which is less admirable. There are some—many perhaps—who are indifferent to the question of life after death, in the sense that they never think about the question at all. Or at least they never think about their own deaths at all. It is surely very common (and I suppose there are good biological reasons for it) to *repress* the thought of one's own death. 'All men are mortal, and I am a man, therefore . . .'; but one does not draw the conclusion, or one assents to it in a purely verbal way. Frederick Myers, it is said, once asked his neighbour at a dinner party, 'What do you think will happen to you after death?' The man replied, 'Oh, I suppose I shall inherit eternal bliss, but I do wish you would not talk about such a depressing subject.' This man surely *was* emotionally concerned about his own death and what would follow it, but was doing his best to repress this emotional concern.

The repression operates not only in the individual, but also at the social level—in the form of a taboo—as indeed this story illustrates. And the taboo, I think, is even stronger now than it was in Myers's day. But a subject which people take care to avoid is not one to which they are indifferent. They avoid it because it concerns them too much. In some people, indeed, this process of 'social conditioning' may have succeeded so well that they never even think about their own deaths. So far as their conscious thoughts and feelings go, they really are indifferent to the question 'Is there life after death or not?'. But this does not show that they have no emotional interest in it or concern about it. Perhaps they do have such an interest or concern, but in a 'repressed' form, below the threshold of consciousness. In support of this view, we may notice that when they refuse to discuss the question of life after death, their refusal has an edge to it, so to speak. It is not that the subject does not interest them, or that they have no anxiety or concern about it, but rather that it is too painful and too alarming to talk about. They prefer to let sleeping dogs lie, and this creature certainly is a dog (perhaps he is the dog Cerberus). He might very well wake up and bite you if you gave him any encouragement.

I conclude, then, that for the majority of human beings, with the possible exception of some mystics, it is very difficult to put their feelings—their emotions and wishes—entirely out of their minds when they consider the problem of life after death. The feelings and wishes are there. Even though some of us have succeeded in 'repressing' them—keeping them out

of consciousness—they are still there, subconsciously or unconsciously.

MOTIVES AND REASONS

If I am right so far, the path of the psychical researcher is
beset with formidable obstacles. The problem of survival—
whatever conclusion he reaches about it—is surely one of the
most important problems he has to consider. Must we infer,
from what I have been saying, that he cannot hope to in-
vestigate it in an unbiased manner? If so, is it at all likely
that he will succeed in solving it?

In this very awkward situation there is only one thing to be
done. We must try to drag our feelings and wishes into the
open, instead of pretending that they are not there. We must
try to find out what we should like to believe about life after
death, and also what we should *not* like to believe. This is not
an easy task. It might very well be that our wishes are by no
means simple—that in some ways we want the Survival
Hypothesis to be true, but in other ways we want it to be
false. Moreover, in a matter of this importance, which touches
each one of us so closely, one person's wishes may well be
quite different from another's.

We should all agree that motives for believing a proposition
are very different from reasons for believing it. Motives for
disbelief too are very different from reasons for disbelief. It is
important to notice that the same applies to the neutral state
of suspense of judgement. Sitting on the fence is a posture which
is very agreeable to some people (I rather enjoy it myself), but
to others it is almost unbearable. In all three cases—belief,
disbelief, and suspense of judgement—we must do our best to
distinguish between motives and reasons; in all three, we must
be clear about the motives if we are to do justice to the reasons.
A juryman, when he is making up his mind what verdict to
give, should be guided by the evidence which has been presented to him. But before considering the evidence, he will do
well to notice and make allowance for the fact that he does

not at all like the prisoner's face, or conversely that he does like it.

<h3>THE FEAR OF HELL</h3>

It is very commonly supposed that in this matter of post-mortem survival all our wishes are on one side: that everybody, always, would like the Survival Hypothesis to be true. It is therefore very commonly said that belief in life after death is 'just wishful thinking'; and even if someone does not go so far as complete belief in life after death, but merely thinks of it as a possibility which should be considered seriously, even he will often be accused of 'wishful thinking'.

I want to suggest that this widely held view is mistaken. There are *motives* for disbelieving in life after death, as well as motives for believing in it. Some people would like the Survival Hypothesis to be true, and if it could be proved to be true, they would be delighted. But others would like it to be false, and if it were ever proved to be true, they would be not only surprised, but dismayed or even horrified: and this not only because they have 'invested their theoretical capital' in a materialistic or naturalistic view of the world, and would have to revise many of their beliefs about the universe and about human personality if the Survival Hypothesis turned out to be true, but also on more personal and so to speak more intimate grounds ('existential' ones, perhaps?). There are people who just do not want to live after death; and if it were to be proved, or even shown to be rather more likely than not, that they will in fact continue to live and have experiences after their physical organisms are dead, they would find the situation quite unbearable.

It is obvious that such people have *motives* for disbelieving in life after death, and I want to suggest that these motives are more powerful than is commonly supposed. They are of several different kinds. One of them is quite simply the fear of Hell. I suspect that this has been an important factor in the steady decline of religious belief during the past three centuries.

According to some religious doctrines, a very large number of persons will find themselves in Hell after they are dead and only a small remnant will be 'saved'. If one considers the matter from a purely selfish point of view, this obviously gives one a very strong motive for wishing *not* to survive death. The chances that one will be among 'the elect' are small; and what sensible person, if he had the choice, would take the risk of undergoing everlasting misery? Nor need one be purely selfish about it. There are motives of charity and compassion as well. If our religious teachers tell us, as they did at one time (not so very long ago), that a very large part of the human race, or even a considerable part—twenty per cent, let us say—will be in a state of everlasting misery after death, surely this gives any charitable person a very strong motive for wishing that there should be *no* life after death? 'O grave, where is thy victory?' Should this be said with exultation, or with lamentation? If the grave did have its victory after all, there would be no everlasting misery for any human being.

Let us remember also that in the history of our Western civilization there have been such things as ecclesiastical tyranny, and political tyranny supported by the ecclesiastical authorities. That is why defenders of human liberty have often been anti-religious as well, and have accepted more or less materialistic theories of human personality which exclude the idea of life after death. For the ultimate sanction of ecclesiastical tyranny was the threat of Hell-fire; and if only one could persuade oneself and one's neighbours that there is no life after death at all, there would be no need to worry about Hell-fire any more.

'ETERNAL BLISS'

Moreover, if someone were fortunate enough to be included among 'the elect', what kind of a life could he look forward to after death? It was described as eternal bliss or everlasting happiness. It is not clear whether the words 'eternal' and 'everlasting' were here being used as synonyms, though I think the ordinary believer did not draw any distinction between them. Perhaps we might 'have it both ways' if we conceived of eternal life as an unending specious present.

Psychologists have pointed out that the present as we experience it in this world is not a 'knife-edge', a line without breadth between past and future. The experienced present, rather misleadingly called 'specious', has a finite though brief duration, and the length of it varies in some degree with the psychological and physiological state of the observer. (If you have ever experienced a road accident or a crash in an air-craft, you probably noticed that everything seemed to be happening very slowly.) This idea of eternal life as an unending specious present seems to be accepted by the philosopher Peter Abelard in his celebrated hymn *O quanta qualia*: 'Illic nec sabbato succedit sabbatum, Perpes laetitia sabbatizantium'.

In the more mystical forms of Christianity, it was wisely said that the nature of this eternal bliss cannot be adequately described in human language. The most one could do was to describe it as 'the vision of God', the loving vision of him who first loved us: no merely private vision either, but a communal or social one, shared by others who love him too and also love us. Could anything be more desirable than this? Indeed nothing could be better, though we cannot hope to conceive in detail what such an experience would be like. 'Eye hath not seen nor ear heard.'

But in the more popular versions of Christian teaching, those which had most influence with the great majority of believers, this wise reticence was neglected, and eternal bliss was represented as an endless succession of religious exercises. It was to be like being in church for ever and ever, singing hymns of praise out of an infinitely long version of *Hymns Ancient and Modern*. No doubt the congregation would contain many very admirable persons, and it would be a pleasure, indeed an honour, to be singing in their company. But it did not seem to occur to religious teachers that a perpetual Sunday morning might become a little tedious after a while. One can have too much of a good thing.

Are we to suppose, then, that after death we have only two alternatives to look forward to—either eternal boredom or eternal misery? No doubt any reasonable person would prefer the first, if he had the choice. Boredom is certainly a lesser evil than acute pain. But surely it is a choice of evils. And so one may come to think that it would be a less disagreeable prospect if there were no life after death at all; or even a positively agreeable prospect, if we think of death as the beginning of 'eternal rest'. We must not underrate the attractions of the idea of 'eternal rest'. There are many people among us who are very tired indeed, and the more complicated our civilization becomes, the more of them there will be.

I know it will be said that these two pictures of life after death—eternal misery for unrepentant wrongdoers and eternal hymn-singing for the elect—were meant to be interpreted symbolically, and not literally. No doubt this is well understood today, both by religious teachers and by their audiences or readers. But was it so in the seventeenth century, or in the eighteenth, or even in the first half of the nineteenth? Was it so in the days of the old-fashioned 'Hell-fire sermons'? Surely they were meant to frighten people, and really did frighten them too. And surely both the preachers and their congregations believed that these terrifying accounts of Hell were literally true, or at least were close approximations to the truth. If any allowance had to be made for the imperfections of human language, the appropriate conclusion would surely be that Hell was even worse than it was painted.

I do not wish to deny that there may be good reasons for the belief in Hell, and good reasons too for preaching Hell-fire sermons. On the contrary, it seems to be likely that if we do live after death, we shall find that the doctrine of Purgatory, at any rate, is substantially true, though I should suppose that Purgatory is to be conceived as a kind of nightmare-like dream rather than a place. But please may I remind you once again that I am not concerned at present with the reasons for holding this or that belief, but only with motives? I am only talking at present about the feelings and wishes, whether favourable or unfavourable, which the thought of life after death arouses; and I have been emphasizing the unfavourable ones because they are very often ignored or forgotten.

AN ALTERNATIVE TO THE CHRISTIAN WORLD-VIEW

It seems pretty clear that attitudes towards life after death in our Western civilization have altered very considerably in the last three and a half centuries. The people I am concerned with in this discussion are those who took religious doctrines seriously and tried to reflect on their implications: not priests or theologians only, but also intelligent laymen. There is a thought which must surely have occurred to many of them: 'How much better it would be if there were no life after death at all! One would gladly give up the hope of Heaven if one could be sure of escaping Hell, and sure too that other people will escape it.' In the sixteenth century and the first half of the seventeenth, most people would no doubt dismiss such a thought from their minds almost as soon as it occurred. They would say to themselves, 'It is absurd to have such wishes. It is quite certain that there is a life after death. There is no possibility of escaping it. So we must face the situation as best we may.' For at that time there did not appear to be any tenable alternatives to the Christian world-view. But already in the second half of the seventeenth century an alternative began to be dimly visible, at least to the highly educated. It was the world-view which we now call 'naturalism' or 'materialism', and it was made possible by the scientific discoveries which began in the late Renaissance period. It began to appear conceivable, or even likely, that all the mental and spiritual attributes of human beings—consciousness, memory, moral character, even saintliness itself—were wholly dependent upon physical processes in the central nervous system, especially the brain. If only one could believe this, the fear of Hell would be abolished once for all. Of course, the hope of Heaven would be abolished too. But, as I have suggested already, Heaven as represented in traditional Christian teaching did not really seem to be so very desirable.

From the eighteenth century onwards, it came to be more and more widely known that there *was* this alternative to orthodox Christian doctrines. And by the second quarter of the twentieth century, with the slow but sure growth of scientific education, and with the visible effects of scientific technology staring all of us in the face, it was realized by almost everyone that the Christian world-view had a very powerful and attractive competitor. The idea that the Christian view of human personality might be entirely mistaken, and that very probably there was no life after death at all—this idea, at one time so strange and shocking, has now seeped down through all the educational levels of our society, and has become perfectly familiar to the man in the bar and the scullery-maid in the kitchen. It has come to be believed, or rather, just taken for granted, by more and more people that there is no need to worry about life after death at all—no reason to hope for it and no reason to fear it.

I may just remind you in passing that it has all happened before, as one may see by reading the great materialist poet Lucretius who lived in the first century B.C. He makes it quite plain that one of the great advantages of a materialist outlook is that it gets rid of our fears of what will happen to us after death. Some of you may remember the splendid but slightly ironical lines which Virgil wrote about him in the *Georgics*:

> Felix qui potuit rerum cognoscere causas,
> atque metus omnis et inexorabile fatum
> Subiecit pedibus, strepitumque Acherontis avari.[1]

You may also remember the remark which someone made to Robespierre: 'Être Suprême, Être Suprême, vous m'ennuyez avec votre Être Suprême.' Something like this has happened

---

[1] *Georgics*, ii. 490–3. 'Happy is he who has been able to know the causes of things, and has trampled beneath his feet all fears, and inexorable Fate, and the roar of greedy Acheron.'

to the idea of life after death. It aroused hopes at one time, and fears too. But now, in the minds of many though not all, it has become a bore; and that, perhaps, is about the worst thing which can happen to any idea.

So much for the fear of Hell; and what I have said about it will apply to the fear of Purgatory too. That is one motive for disbelieving in life after death. But still, it is only a motive for disbelieving in one particular version of the survival hypothesis, the traditional Christian version. In Spiritualist doctrines, so far as I am acquainted with them, or at least in the most popular versions of them, very little, if anything, is said about Hell; and it is not maintained (as it is, or used to be, in some versions of Protestant Christianity) that only a small minority of the human race will be 'saved'. On the contrary, the ordinary decent man with no pretensions to sanctity seems to have quite a good time in the Next World, if we accept what we are told in mediumistic communications.

Even so, we do hear something of the expiation which has to be made in the Next World for selfishness or unkindness in this one; and we are told that until the expiation has been made, the discarnate spirit cannot rise from the lower and darker spheres to the higher and brighter ones. This amounts to saying that even in this moderately cheerful picture of life after death, there is still a place for Purgatory or something substantially like it. It seems to me (and I say it with fear and trembling) that in any plausible version of the Survival Hypothesis we shall have to suppose that something like the old religious doctrine of 'rewards and punishments' after death is true. We need not indeed suppose that the rewards and punishments are assigned to us by an external judge, as they are in the traditional pictures of the 'Great Assize',[1] but rather

---

[1] e.g. in the hymn *Dies Irae*:

> Judex ergo cum sedebit
> Quidquid latet apparebit,
> Nil inultum remanebit.

that the sort of world which a discarnate personality experiences after death corresponds to the habitual thoughts and wishes of that personality, including thoughts and wishes which were unconscious or repressed in earthly life. 'Each goes to his own place', and 'birds of a feather flock together'.

Moreover, these communications suggest, I think, that if we do live after death, the terrifying words in the Gospel[1] may turn out to be true: 'Thou shalt by no means come out thence, till thou hast paid the uttermost farthing.'

So much for what Hamlet called 'the dread of something after death'. No doubt this dread is far less common now than it was in the days of the old 'Hell-fire' sermons. You may remember that David Hume, who had had to listen to a good many of them, concluded that people 'took pleasure in being terrified'. This might seem paradoxical. The explanation was, he thought, that they did not fully believe what they were told, because the Next World, as the preachers described it, was so very unlike this one. I wonder whether he was right. I would suggest, on the contrary, that the fear of post-mortem punishment still has some force even now, especially among reflective people, and still gives them quite a strong motive for disbelief in life after death.

There is another motive for disbelief in it which is difficult to discuss and perhaps I should apologize for mentioning it at all. There are people who 'find everything too much for them'. They are in a state of almost constant fatigue. You may remember the story of the overworked charwoman who was asked what her idea of Heaven was. 'Doing nothing for ever and ever', she said. What she wanted and hoped to have after death was a state of unending rest, everlasting repose. She probably did not realize that this was just what she was going to have, if the materialistic conception of human personality should turn out to be correct. For in that case, dying really would be very like going to sleep and never waking up again, and from then onwards there would be no possibility of doing anything. So although she probably did not know it,

[1] Matt. 5: 26.

she had a very strong motive for disbelief in life after death. I must confess that I have some sympathy with her; and I suspect that there are a good many persons who agree with her, though they might be reluctant to admit it.

It is very commonly supposed that the belief in life after death is the most obvious of all examples of 'wishful thinking' —believing something highly improbable merely because one wishes it to be true. My answer to this is 'it depends who you are, and what state of mind or body you are in at the time'. It might very well be that some of those who *dis*believe in life after death are 'wishful thinkers' too.

'PREPARE TO MEET THY GOD'

Many years ago, in a library which had belonged to my grandfather, I came across a little book, written in the eighteenth century. I had never heard of the author before, and I greatly regret that I cannot now remember his name or the title of his book. He was an ingenious person, obviously influenced by the epistemology of Locke. His aim was to reconcile two religious doctrines which seem at first sight to be incompatible with each other. According to the one, a clergyman would say to a dying person 'Prepare to meet thy God'; and this implies, or at least seems to imply, that the post-mortem Judgement will occur immediately after death. But according to the other, and equally orthodox, doctrine the deceased person will 'sleep in his grave', perhaps for many centuries, before the post-mortem Judgement occurs. He will have to wait until the General Resurrection on the Last Day. One might be inclined to think that this second doctrine is a little more comforting than the first; for there will at any rate be a period of repose, probably quite a long one, between death and the Judgement.

The author argued, however, that if one considers the empirical cash-value of these two doctrines, there is in fact no difference between them. From the point of view of the deceased person, both of them come to exactly the same thing.

For a person who is in a state of dreamless sleep, no matter how long it lasts in physical time, there is no experienced time-lapse at all. So for him it is as if the Judgement occurred immediately after death. He loses consciousness, and then 'the next thing he knows' is that he is standing before God's judgement seat. Therefore the clergyman is quite right when he says to a dying person 'Prepare to meet thy God'. From the dying person's point of view it will be as if the Judgement occurs immediately, as soon as he is dead.

PETER PRICE

I cannot resist mentioning a tradition which has been handed down in my own family. This too concerns the empiricist eighteenth century. At that time they lived just inside the border of Wales, at Newtown in Montgomeryshire. Like other families who lived in rather remote parts of the country, which were not much affected by the Reformation, they were Roman Catholics. An ancestor of mine, Peter Price, who was then the head of the family, had a long and serious illness and as a result he was unconscious for some days. When he had recovered consciousness, he described an experience which he had had. He said he had visited the Next World and had seen for himself that what the priests said about it was quite incorrect. In the light of this empirical falsification, he gave up his Catholic beliefs and persuaded his family to do the same. Some years later he visited America, and on the way there he encountered a Quaker, with whom he had many theological conversations. Attracted no doubt by the doctrine of the Inner Light, with its emphasis on first-hand experience, he became a Quaker himself and persuaded his family to do likewise; and some of my relatives are Quakers to this day. I cannot help feeling a little proud of being a descendant of one who attached so much importance to the concept of empirical falsification.

'YOU OUGHT NOT TO HAVE STARTED FROM HERE'

I have been assuming all along, as you see, that the question whether there is life after death is a question of fact, even though at present we do not have sufficient evidence to settle it. The evidence now available to us points both ways. The evidence offered by the biological sciences suggests rather strongly that the Survival Hypothesis is false. The paranormal evidence suggests rather strongly that it is true. But perhaps some of you may think that this assumption of mine is fundamentally mistaken. You may remember the story of the man who got lost in a town which he had never visited before. At last, in desperation, he stopped a passer-by and asked him for directions. The reply he received was, 'You ought not to have started from here.' If you start by asking the wrong question you cannot very well expect to find the right answer. According to such critics (and perhaps nearly all of you will agree with them) my mistaken starting-point was this: I have been assuming that the question we wish to answer is a question about the *duration* of our conscious existence. Does it continue after our physical organisms are dead? Perhaps we cannot answer the question once for all, but might we not find some empirical evidence which is relevant to it? It seems to me that we can. The paranormal evidence does give some support to the Survival Hypothesis.

QUALITY AND DURATION

But the critics I have in mind will say that questions about the *duration* of our conscious existence are irrelevant. If I do not misunderstand them (which I probably do, for their views seem to me highly paradoxical) they wish to draw the sharpest possible distinction between two adjectives which have often been used as if they were synonyms: 'eternal' on the one hand and 'everlasting' on the other. Their contention is that the word 'eternal' denotes a quality and has no temporal implications at all. Eternal life is just life of the highest possible quality, $a+$ life, so to speak. Its duration, be it great or little, is irrelevant. I suppose it would be bound to have *some* duration, if it is to count as 'life' at all. But still, as the Psalmist put it, 'One day in thy courts is better than a thousand'; better, that is, than a thousand days elsewhere. And indeed any religious person, or any theistically religious person at any rate, would agree that one day in the Lord's courts *is* better than a thousand days elsewhere. But surely he would also think that a thousand days in the Lord's courts are better still?

It is no doubt possible to have 'too much of a good thing'. A fortnight's holiday is good, but a year's holiday might be far too long. But is this still true when the 'good thing' is the very best of all possible good things?

Moreover, if 'eternal life' just means 'life of the highest possible quality', it would follow that 'eternal misery' is a self-contradictory concept. It would therefore be absurd to take any steps to avoid eternal misery. 'Beware of the dog.' One need not pay much attention to this warning if it is logically impossible that dogs should exist. On the contrary, it is only too likely that this dog does exist. Beware of him, because he has a very nasty bite indeed: and if you do not take care, he might go on biting you *in saecula saeculorum*.

I hope I am not being unfair to those who insist that the word 'eternal' in the phrase 'eternal life' just denotes a quality and has no reference at all to duration. Their motive is an admirable one. Any religious person must have noticed how many there are among us who think that the 'good news' of the Gospel (τὸ εὐαγγέλιον) is too good to be true.

What makes them think so? Not the ethical teachings of the Gospel. Agnostics and humanists are willing to accept the precept 'Thou shalt love thy neighbour as thyself', and they do their best to put it into practice too. Some of them are even willing to sacrifice their lives for their neighbour's sake, although they are convinced that life in this world is the only life they have; and if any state of mind is wholly admirable, surely this one is. Surely we do not wish, and ought not to wish, to antagonize such persons? They are on our side, whether they know it or not. So let us forget about the most paradoxical part of our 'good news', the part which concerns 'the life of the world to come' (can we quite believe it ourselves?) and then all men of good will can work together for the good of all mankind. To achieve this very desirable end, all we have to do is to alter the concept of 'eternal life' just a little, by drawing a distinction between the two adjectives 'eternal' and 'everlasting'. So let us say that by 'eternal life' we just mean 'life of the highest possible quality', however long—or short—its duration may be.

But perhaps it might also be desirable to remember the Gospel precept 'Agree with thine adversary quickly'. For if we stick to this naïve and all-too-literal hope of everlasting life after death, our churches, and our chapels too, will soon be empty, and the Christian religion will fade away through sheer lack of adherents. That has happened before, and to very admirable religions too: Mithraism, for instance, or the Neoplatonized version of Greco-Roman polytheism which the Emperor Julian tried in vain to save some sixteen centuries ago.

I would suggest, however, that those who wish to recommend a watered-down version of Christianity, in which the very idea of life after death is left out, are making a psychological mistake. They assume that it is easier to accept a simple creed than a complex one. That might be true if 'accepting' just means 'giving intellectual assent to . . .'. But religion is something more than giving intellectual assent to propositions, however important those propositions may be. It is a 'way of life'. It affects our thoughts and feelings and wishes at many different points. Its complexity is essential to it. There are commandments which we should act upon. There are petitions we should make. There are emotions we should try to cultivate: forgiveness, for example, when someone has been unkind or unfair to us, resignation to God's will for us, trust in his love when we lose someone very dear to us, and trust too in his love for the one we have lost. Moreover, if we find it very difficult indeed to have these emotional attitudes, we are to ask for God's grace to enable us to have them. You will recall the prayer of St. Augustine, 'Da quod iubes et iube quod vis'.

If I am not mistaken, one eminent theologian has said that the very idea of life after death is unacceptable to *biologisch denkende Leute*: and surely in these days no educated person can avoid thinking about human personality 'in a biological way'? Barring unfortunate accidents, the amoeba, the simplest of all living organisms, may continue to live for a very long time; but obviously this cannot be true of very complex organisms like ourselves. So if the Christian religion is to continue, surely we must be careful to distinguish between the quality of our lives on the one hand, and their duration on the other? Even from a purely secular point of view, a short life and a happy one is far better than a long and miserable one; and surely any religious person would agree that three score and ten years 'with' God (or even two score years), followed by complete extinction, would be far better than an endless life 'without' him? 'One day in thy courts' is better than a thousand elsewhere.

As you see, I agree that we must accept this distinction between the quality of a person's life and its duration. If it be indeed true that each of us can look forward to a life which is literally endless ('everlasting'), that is not necessarily a happy prospect at all. For very good and charitable persons, it may be a happy prospect, and one must admit that such persons are surprisingly numerous (at any rate it always surprises me). But what are we to think if we ourselves are not included among them?

It seems to me that if we fall short of this rather high standard, we have a strong motive for wishing that the doctrine of life after death should be false. If the kind of life we have after death depends upon our moral characters, as it surely must if there is life after death at all—if it be true that 'thou shalt by no means escape thence, till thou hast paid the uttermost farthing'—then there are few among us who can hope for a wholly happy time in the world to come. And who would dare to say that he is one of them? The ideal situation, from this point of view, would be that very good and charitable people should continue to live *ad infinitum* after death, and that others should just cease to exist when their bodies die: eternal bliss for the good, eternal sleep for the others.

But if we accept the teachings of Christianity, or indeed the teachings of any of the higher religions, we have to admit that this combination of prospects is just the one which is most unlikely to be realized. If there is life after death at all, it must surely be something which is, as it were, inherent in the nature of human personality, no matter what one's moral character is. The only probable alternatives are that either everyone continues to live after death or that no one does.

DIES IRAE

I conclude that for very many of us it would be a mistake to think that the idea of life after death is a comforting one. It depends who you are, and what kind of moral character you have. For very good and charitable persons, it may indeed be a comforting one. But what are we to think if we are not included among them? If wishes could decide the question 'Is there life after death?' and it were put to the vote, it is by no means certain that the Ayes would have it.

You will remember the terrifying words in the hymn *Dies Irae*:

> Quid sum miser tum dicturus,
> Quem patronum rogaturus,
> Quum vix justus sit securus?

We need not suppose, as the writer of *Dies Irae* did, that the post-mortem judgement will be postponed until 'the end of the world'; and even if it is, there might still be no *experienced* time-interval between death and 'the Last Day'. In that case, as I have suggested already, for each of us it will be as if the Judgement occurs immediately after death.

But the writer's question 'Quid sum miser tum dicturus ... ?'
still arises; and he answers it in a surprising way, by making
an appeal to the Judge himself:

> Recordare, Jesu pie,
> Quod sum causa tuae viae;
> Ne me perdas illa die.
>
> Quaerens me sedisti lassus,
> Redemisti crucem passus,
> Tantus labor non sit cassus.

The Judge is himself the Redeemer; and that, perhaps, is
the most important part of the 'good news' of the Gospel, τὸ
εὐαγγέλιον. Christianity is a religion of redemption.

6

TWO CONCEPTIONS OF THE NEXT WORLD

I F we have been brought up in the traditions of Protestant Christianity, the ideas of Heaven and Hell are likely to be the first ones which come into our minds when we ask ourselves what life after death might conceivably be like. The strong emotional resistance which many people nowadays feel against the very idea of life after death may well have something to do with traditional ideas of Heaven and Hell. To some of you our present this-wordly or secularistic outlook, and the conception of human personality which goes with it (the theory sometimes called 'psychosomatic monism'), may seem a very depressing one. So it is in some ways. But it does have the important emotional advantage of delivering people from the burden of Hell, which has oppressed the lives of many generations. I think we hardly realize now how heavy that burden must have been.

People who believe in life after death, and even people who are willing to discuss the subject at all, are often accused of 'wishful thinking'. It is worth while to remember that disbelievers in life after death may be wishful thinkers too.[1] In the controversy concerning life after death there are wishful thinkers on both sides; and on both sides some of the wishes may be quite respectable ones.

Psychical researchers, however, are not very much concerned with the ideas of Heaven and Hell. Possibly the ideas of Paradise and Purgatory do just fall within their field of interest. But Heaven, which is supposed to be a state of 'bliss inexpressible', is surely not a state into which any ordinary

[1] Cf. above, pp. 82 ff.

human being is likely to pass immediately after death; and the same applies to Hell, which is supposed to be a state of inexpressible misery. Questions about Heaven are not questions about the Next World, but about the next but one or the next but two; and the same applies, I think, to questions about Hell.

But in this discussion we *are* concerned with the Next World, the one into which we are supposed to pass immediately after death. We have to ask ourselves what the Next World might conceivably be like, in order to understand the concept of survival itself. For it is personal survival which we have to discuss; and if one's personal existence does continue after the disintegration of the physical organism, there must be *experiences* of some kind or other after death; and we must try to consider what kind of experiences they might be. A surviving person must be aware of something if he is to continue to be a person: and there must be something in his post-mortem experience which plays roughly the same part as our perceived physical environment plays now. So we must ask what kind of a 'world', or approximation to a world, he might be aware of.

If I am right so far, the idea of personal life after death *is*, among other things, the idea of a 'Next World'; and we must have something to say about the idea of a next world, if we are willing to discuss the Survival Hypothesis at all.

I do not wish to suggest that for this purpose it is necessary to believe that there *is* a Next World. There are distinguished psychical researchers, Professor E. R. Dodds, for instance, who reject the Survival Hypothesis altogether.[1] All I am claiming at the moment is that the idea of a Next World or 'Another World' is an integral part of the Survival Hypothesis itself, and must therefore be considered by anyone who is willing to consider the Survival Hypothesis.

What shall we say of the Next World but one, or the next but two? In some theories of life after death, it is supposed

---

[1] 'Why I Do Not Believe in Survival', *Proceedings of the Society for Psychical Research*, 42 (1934), 147–72.

that we do not remain for ever in the world in which we find ourselves immediately after death, but 'move on' after a while into another. First we are in Purgatory, then in Paradise and finally (perhaps) in Heaven: and in some theories of life after death it is supposed that there are seven Heavens, the seventh being the 'highest' one of all. The 'movement' from one of these after-death worlds to another must not, however, be conceived of as a change of place, but rather as a change of consciousness.

The idea of the Next World but one, or the next but two, had better be left to saints or theologians or whoever you think the appropriate experts are. For my part, I am willing to listen respectfully to what these experts say. But I do not think I am qualified to discuss what they have to tell us. So let us fix our attention on the idea of the Next World, and consider how we might try to conceive of it.

On the face of it, there are two different ways of conceiving of the Next World, and they correspond to two different conceptions of survival itself.

First there is what I shall call the *embodied* conception of survival, and secondly there is the *disembodied* conception of it. According to the first, personality (or finite personality at any rate) cannot possibly exist without some kind of embodiment. At death a person loses his physical body. So, after death, he must have a body of some other kind, composed of some 'higher' kind of matter which is not perceptible by means of our present physical sense-organs. Those who accept this conception of survival usually maintain that each of us does in fact have such a 'higher' body even in this present life, as well as a physical body, and that even in this life the two bodies may occasionally be separated, in the 'out of the body' experiences which are sometimes reported.

According to the second or 'disembodied' conception of survival, what survives death is just the mind or spirit, and this is regarded as a wholly immaterial entity. Its essential attributes are consciousness, memory, volition, and the capacity for having emotions. It would of course be admitted that in this present life there is constant interaction between the immaterial soul and the material organism. But at death this interaction ceases; indeed, on this view death just *is* the termination of soul–body interaction, and afterwards the soul is supposed to exist and to have experiences in a completely disembodied state.

In this theory there is a kind of ambivalent attitude towards the body. From one point of view, the material organism is the *instrument* of the immaterial soul. By means of this instrument, the soul is able to get information about the material world through the sense-organs, and is also able in some small degree to control material objects in accordance with its desires. At death, the soul is deprived of this useful instrument. Without it, how lamentable the soul's condition must be.[1]

But from another point of view, emphasized by the Pythagoreans and by some of the Platonists, the material organism could be regarded as the prison of the soul which prevents it from exercising its full powers and compels it to undergo all sorts of painful and humiliating experiences. No doubt these experiences have a disciplinary value, and may even be indispensable for the soul's development. Still, it is better to be out of prison than in it. Some of the Pythagoreans even said that the body is the tomb of the soul ($\sigma\tilde{\omega}\mu\alpha$ $\sigma\tilde{\eta}\mu\alpha$). The same view may be expressed more moderately by saying that this world is a place of exile;[2] our true home is elsewhere in some 'higher' world than this. 'My heart's in the Highlands, my heart is not here.'

---

[1] Cf. the little poem which the Emperor Hadrian addressed to his soul when he was dying:

> Animula vagula blandula,
> Hospes comesque corporis,
> Quae nunc abibis in loca,
> Pallidula, rigida, nudula,
> Nec ut soles dabis jocos?

[2] 'et ad Jerusalem e Babylonia / Post longa regredi tandem exilia' (Peter Abelard, *O quanta qualia*).

EMBODIED SURVIVAL

Corresponding to these two different conceptions of survival, there are two different conceptions of the Next World. If we accept the embodied conception of survival, we have to think of the Next World as a kind of material world, the environment of the quasi-material body which the surviving personality is supposed to have. It would be a material world in the sense that it has spatial attributes. The space of the Next World might conceivably have more than three dimensions, and its geometry need not necessarily be Euclidean. But concepts such as 'shape', 'size', 'location', and 'motion' would have to apply to it. It would also be necessary, I think, that the objects which make up such a world should have what philosophers call 'secondary qualities'. The secondary qualities with which we are familiar in this present life are colour, sound, smell, temperature, hardness, softness, etc. We need not suppose that precisely the same qualities exist in the Next World, but we should have to suppose that qualities analogous to them do. Finally, we should have to suppose that objects in the Next World have causal properties of some kind, whereby they can cause changes in one another. In this present world we are familiar with many different sorts of causal properties, for example weight, elasticity, rigidity, solubility, electric charge. We need not suppose that precisely the same ones exist in other-worldly objects; but we *should* have to suppose that other-worldly objects have causal properties of some kind.

According to this conception of it, the Next World would still be some kind of material world, however different it might be in detail from the material world with which we are now familiar; and it is well known that in many mediumistic communications the Next World *is* described as if it were a kind of material world. Indeed, in some of them it seems to be surprisingly similar to this present world in which we now live. The same could be said of descriptions of the Next World (or Worlds) in religious traditions. For instance, in the pre-Reformation Christian tradition Paradise was represented as a kind of garden or park; and this is indeed the literal meaning of the word παράδεισος, which the Greeks borrowed from the Persians.

THE NEXT WORLD IN *AENEID* BOOK VI

Now this quasi-material conception of the Next World is faced with an obvious difficulty. If the Next World is a spatial world, where is it? In one of the most celebrated passages in ancient classical literature, the sixth book of Virgil's *Aeneid*, we are told about Aeneas' visit to the Next World, under the guidance of the Sibyl of Cumae. Apparently they walked there.[1]

I suggest that we may take all this as a description of a visionary experience of some kind, and perhaps this is what the illustrious poet intended. The Sibyl was a mediumistic lady, and Virgil begins the story with a vivid description of the physical symptoms of her mediumistic trance.[2] But if we take the narrative in that way, we are changing over to *another* conception of the Next World—the 'dream-like' conception of it, which I shall discuss later. So for the moment let us take the story just as we find it, and consider its implications.

We can hardly believe that the River Styx and the Elysian Fields are somewhere in the bowels of the earth. But still, the difficulty is not insuperable. It is true that the Next World, according to this conception of it, is a spatial world. But it need not be located anywhere in the physical space with which we are now familiar. It is conceivable that there are many different spaces in the universe, different in the sense that they have no spatial relations to one another. Alternatively, it might be suggested that there is only one space in the universe, but that it has other dimensions in addition to the three which our present senses make us aware of. According to this inter-pretation, the Sibyl used her paranormal powers to enable

---

[1] *Aeneid*, vi. 263, 268.
[2] Ibid., vi. 45–51, 77–80.

Aeneas (and herself) to be aware of this other space, or of these other and normally imperceptible dimensions of our familiar physical space. They did not literally *go* anywhere. What happened to them was a change of consciousness.

DISEMBODIED SURVIVAL

Let us now turn to the other conception of survival, what I called the 'disembodied' conception of it. If we take this view of survival, it is not easy to see at first sight how there could be a Next *World* at all. What kind of experiences could a wholly immaterial soul be supposed to have? As it has no sense-organs of any sort, surely it will have to spend the whole of its time in pure thought, contemplating the *a priori* truths of logic and mathematics which are independent of the data of the senses? Such a conception of the after-life may seem to many people exceedingly dreary and unsatisfying, however satisfactory it might be to logicians and mathematicians like Descartes. Of course, we might have to put up with it whether it satisfied us or not. If we do exist in a completely disembodied state after death, and if it is really true that a completely disembodied soul or spirit can have no experiences at all except purely intellectual ones, we must just make the best of it, however unsatisfying such an after-life may seem to us.

But I do not think that the disembodied conception of survival really does have these rather unwelcome implications. It is true that a completely disembodied soul would have no sense-organs and therefore no sense-experiences. But it would still have *memory*. Indeed, it must, if there is personal survival at all. Without this, a surviving personality could not retain its personal identity; the surviving entity could not be the same person as the late Mr. Robinson who formerly lived in Church Street, Kensington, and worked in the Westminster Bank. Unless we 'take our memories with us' when we leave the physical body, there can be no *personal* survival at all. For the same reason, we must 'take' our characters with us too—the emotional and conative dispositions which we have acquired during our embodied life on earth. Otherwise we shall not continue to be the same persons after death as we were before. Let us suppose that in our disembodied state we also retain the power of imagination, even though we lose the capacity for having sense-experiences.

A WORLD OF MENTAL IMAGES

On these assumptions, it is not too difficult to form some idea of what the Next World might be like according to the 'disembodied' conception of survival. The obvious suggestion is that it would be a kind of *dream-world*: or to put it the other way round, the dreams we have in this present life would be a kind of foretaste of the experiences we might expect to have after death. In dreams we are cut off from sensory stimuli. The sense-organs cease to operate. But this does not at all prevent us from having experiences, sometimes very vivid and exciting ones. The perceptible objects we are aware of when awake are replaced by mental images, and these mental images are the product of our own memories and desires. If we retain our memories and desires after death (and there can be no personal survival unless we do) these memories and desires may continue to manifest themselves by means of mental images, as they do in this present life when we are dreaming. Life after death on this view would be a kind of dream from which we never wake up.

In this present life we wake up eventually from our dreams. After a time the sense-organs begin to operate again. The dream-images fade away, and we are forced to attend again to our physical environment. Our nose is applied to the grindstone once more, whether we like it or not. But suppose we could no longer wake up. Suppose that someone's sense-organs ceased to operate altogether because his body had died. Then he would just go on dreaming. He would have passed from this world to the Other World or the Next World. This 'passage' from the one world to the other would not of course be a change of place. It would be a change of consciousness, somewhat like the one which occurs now when we fall asleep and begin to dream, except that this time the change would be irreversible. Henceforth the disembodied mind or soul would live wholly in a world constructed out of its own memories and desires.

Here it is important to remember that many of our dream-images are spatial entities. If our dream is of the visual type (as most people's dreams probably are) our dream-images have shape, size, and position; at any rate they have position in relation to one another. If you dream of a mountain land-scape, for instance, there may be an image of a spiky-topped mountain on the left, and an image of a round-topped mountain on the right, with a torrent flowing down between them. But though these dream-images have spatial properties, they are not located in *physical* space. From the point of view of the physicist or geographer these images are nowhere, because no position can be assigned to any of them in a map of the physical universe. They are spatial entities, but the space in which they are is not physical space. They are in a space of their own.

Next, we may notice that such an image-world would appear perfectly real to the disembodied soul itself, as dream-objects usually do now when we are actually dreaming. We only call them 'unreal' by contrast with the world we are aware of when we wake up again. But if we no longer had any waking perception to contrast them with, we should no longer regard them as 'unreal'.

We are sometimes told in mediumistic communications that many discarnate personalities are at first unable to realize that they are dead. This, I think, is perfectly credible on the view of the Next World which we are now discussing. The memories and desires of these newly deceased persons would supply them with images of the same old familiar scenes, and it might not be at all easy for them to discover that what they are now aware of is no longer the physical world, but a world of vivid and coherent mental images. Among these images there might be one which closely resembled the physical body which the discarnate person had when he was alive. He might have a 'dream-body', so to speak, as well as a dream-environment.

In time, however, he might gradually discover that the *causal laws* which apply to the world he is now experiencing are rather different from those he was familiar with in earthly life. He might notice, for instance, that if he desires to be in a certain place, he instantaneously finds himself in it, without passing through any intermediate places on the way; or that when he thinks of something, it immediately presents itself before him in a visible form. He would then be driven to the conclusion that he is no longer in the physical world after all. For though the objects he is aware of might closely resemble physical objects in having shapes, sizes, colours, etc. (as dream-objects often do now), it would gradually become clear to him that the causal laws which apply to them are not the laws of physics, but are much more like the laws of psychology.

Conceivably a *very* dogmatic materialist might never succeed in realizing that he was dead and in the Other World. He might prefer to believe that he had been transported to another planet. It might even be (as I think is asserted in some mediumistic communications) that a very firm disbelief in survival would prevent the surviving personality from having any post-mortem experiences at all. Then he would never know that he had survived, because he preferred not to know. But I should suppose that this result would be unlikely if his disbelief in survival was of a purely theoretical kind, without any strong desire or emotion to reinforce it.

A SUBJECTIVE OTHER WORLD?

It may seem at first sight that such an image-world as I have described would be something purely subjective, and that each discarnate personality would be confined as it were to his own private dream, without any means of contact with other discarnate personalities. Perhaps the Next World of a *very* self-centred person really is like that: a pretty terrifying prospect, if you come to think of it, and as we shall see later, the belief in life after death is by no means a wholly comforting one.

But though on the theory we are discussing there would certainly have to be *many* Next Worlds (not the same one for all) it does not really follow that each of them would be wholly private. Telepathy must be taken into account. Even in this present life telepathic dreams are not infrequent, and there are also occasional telepathic hallucinations. In this present life, it is likely that many telepathically received impressions fail to reach consciousness at all, owing to the pressure of biological needs which force us to pay attention to our physical environment. In a disembodied state, this inhibiting influence would be removed. So there might be a common image-world which is the joint product of many telepathically interacting personalities.

Nevertheless, there would still be *many* Next Worlds and not just one. The material world in which we live now has what one might call 'unrestricted publicity'. In principle, any macroscopic object in it can be observed by anyone, provided that he moves his body to the appropriate place and has the normal equipment of sense-organs. But in the universe as a whole, perhaps this unrestricted publicity is something rather exceptional.

Another—and connected—characteristic of the material world, is that in it people with very different moral characters are intermingled, so to speak, and saints and sinners can rub shoulders with one another. Perhaps this is rather exceptional too. For in the next life, if there is one, it is to be expected that only *like-minded* personalities will share a common world— personalities whose memories and desires are sufficiently similar to allow of continuous telepathic interaction. If so, each group of like-minded personalities would have a different next world, public to all the members of that particular group but private to the group as a whole. Each 'goes to his own place' and 'birds of a feather flock together'. Something of this kind is asserted in many religious traditions. You will remember the 'great gulf fixed' between the Next World of

Lazarus and the Next World of Dives in the Gospel parable.[1]
The 'great gulf', I suggest, was a consequence of the *un*like-
mindedness between Dives and those like-minded with him,
on the one hand, and Lazarus and those like-minded with him,
on the other. Between these two groups of persons, there could
be no telepathic interaction.

THE TWO THEORIES COMPARED

Let us now compare these two theories of the Next World.
According to the first, which corresponds with the 'embodied'
conception of survival, the Next World is a quasi-physical
world, though not located in physical space. According to the
second, which corresponds with the 'disembodied' conception
of survival, it is a world of mental images produced by the
memories and desires of the surviving personalities. I hope I
have succeeded in showing that both these theories are more
or less intelligible and coherent, and that both of them deserve
serious consideration.

I expect that most of you prefer the first theory, the quasi-
physical theory which goes with the embodied conception of
survival. A dream-like Next World composed of nothing but
mental images may seem to you somehow 'thin' and unsatisfying. We may emphasize, as I did, that a world of mental
images need not be purely private. A number of like-minded
personalities, who interact telepathically with each other,
could have a common image-world. Again, we may insist, as
I also did, that an image-world could be just as orderly and
coherent as this present material world in which we now live,
though its causal laws would be different from the laws of
physics. But even so, I suspect you will still find this theory
somehow unsatisfying, however agreeable it may seem to a
professional philosopher.

Of course, even though it is unsatisfying, it may be all that
we are going to get. Assuming we survive, we may have to
put up with a dream-like existence after death, even though

[1] Luke 16: 26.

many of us would prefer something different. But I think that behind this feeling of dissatisfaction there is an important point of principle which needs to be brought into the open and stated explicitly. It is a point about the concept of personality itself. It might be argued that a person has to have a body in order to be a person: or at any rate that a *finite* person has to have a body. (We are not concerned here with the infinite personality of God.)

EMBODIMENT AND SOCIAL RELATIONS

Why does a person need a body? (It is a philosopher's business to consider silly questions like this, which sensible adults do not ask, though tiresome children might.) As I have said already, the Pythagoreans, and some of the Platonists, thought that the body is a kind of prison and that it is better to be completely disembodied. For surely one would rather be out of prison than in it? Were they mistaken? In this present life a person *must* have a body, in order to perceive and act upon his physical environment. But though he does need a body while he is in this world, why should he need one in the next?

The answer which is at the back of people's minds (though seldom explicitly stated) is that a person needs a body in order to be a *social* being. It might be argued that no one can be a person unless he has social relations with other persons. According to Christian theism, the most important of all social relationships is the relation of loving, and no one can be a person unless he is at least capable of being related in this way to other persons.

Let us consider this 'social dimension' of personality. There are two different reasons why a social being needs a body. To understand what they are, we have to think of the body not as an anatomist or physiologist thinks of it, but rather as a painter or a dramatist thinks of it. First, it is a means by which inner states of mind *express* themselves in some overt and perceptible manner. To put it rather extravagantly: in order to be a person you must have a *face* which other persons can look at, and recognize and respond to. You do not absolutely need to be able to talk; but if you cannot talk, you do need to be able to make expressive gestures. It comes to this: without some means of expressing oneself one cannot enter into social relations at all. And one function of the body is to provide a person with means of expressing himself.

But it has another function as well. In order to enter into social relations of a permanent kind (friendship, for example) a person has to be recognizable—recognizable, for instance, as the *same* 'Dear old So-and-so' whom you met years ago. Unless persons remained recognizable over considerable periods of time, no such relations as love or friendship would be possible, though very evanescent social relations—of what you might call the 'sherry party' sort—could no doubt exist. And how can a person be recognizable unless he has a body, by means of which he can be identified as the same person whom one met previously?

It follows from this that if a newly dead person is to be recognized by his friends who are in the Next World already, his post-mortem body must resemble his former physical body fairly closely, at least so far as its outward appearance goes. To speak extravagantly again, he must have more or less the same face as he had in his earthly life.

Similarly, if he in his turn is to recognize his friends in the Next World, their post-mortem bodies must not be too different in outward appearance from those they had when he previously knew them in earthly life, though there might be minor differences (comparable to those between the body one has at the age of twenty and the body one has at the age of sixty). Internally, the post-mortem body might be quite different from the physical body, but outwardly it must *look like* the physical body, as of course the occultists and the spiritualists say it does.

The body then is not the prison of the soul, or at any rate that is not all it is. It is the means by which the soul expresses itself and makes itself recognizable to others.

AN IMAGE-BODY

I think these considerations do suggest that *personal* existence, in anything like the form we in which know it now, requires that one should be in some way embodied. But it does not follow from this that the image-theory of the Next World must be mistaken. Here let me remind you again that the body we are discussing now is the body as the artist conceives of it—the painter or the dramatist—and not the body as the anatomist or physiologist conceives of it. The conception of disembodied survival might still be correct, if one thinks of embodiment in the way that anatomists and physiologists do. In order to be a person (or at any rate to be a finite person) one needs to have some sort of body; and it must be not too unlike one's physical body in outward appearance, if one is to be recognizable by others as being the same person after death as one was before. But it need not have anything at all like the complicated internal mechanism which the physical body has. It need not have any internal mechanism, so long as it serves the essential function of expressing one's mental states, and enabling one to be recognized by others. One must have a face, but one need not have a skull, or a cerebral cortex.

Now it seems to me that an *image*-body could perform these functions perfectly well. In order to perform them, it does have to be a spatial entity. But as we have seen already, mental images do have spatial properties, though they are not located in physical space. It is also true that one's body has to be a public entity—public, that is, to all those other persons with whom one has social relations. But as we have also seen, a world of mental images could have some degree of publicity, if we suppose that it is the joint product of the memories and desires of a number of telepathically interacting personalities. It is true that in such an image-world one could not have social relations with *all* the other personalities that there are, but only with those who are sufficiently like-minded with oneself. If one were a very nasty person indeed (exceedingly self-centred or very cruel) one might have to share one's Next

World with only a very few others. But I think that if there is life after death at all, we have to suppose that there are many Next Worlds and not just a single one which is common to all of us, regardless of the different memories, emotions, and desires which each of us brings with him when he gets there.

THE TWO THEORIES 'CONVERGE'

You will remember that at the beginning of the discussion I contrasted two different conceptions of survival, and two correspondingly different conceptions of the Next World: on the one hand, the embodied conception of survival and the quasi-physical theory of the Next World which goes with it; on the other, the disembodied conception of survival, and the dream-like or mental-image-like conception of the Next World which goes with it.

We now begin to suspect that this contrast is not quite so sharp as it seemed at first sight. For it turns out that in the disembodied conception of survival there is room for some sort of body after all;[1] and a Next World composed of mental images, if it has at least some degree of publicity, is less dream-like and less subjective than it seemed at first.

Indeed, I am inclined to think that these two theories of the Next World, which seem so very different, are complementary rather than opposed. They start as it were from opposite ends, but perhaps when both are worked out fully, they meet in the middle.

When we try to think of the Next World, all we can do is to start from analogies suggested by our experiences in this present life. In the first theory which I discussed, we start from a *physical* analogy and try to stretch it as far as we can. We conceive of the Next World on the model of the material world with which we are now familiar, and make any adjustments which seem necessary, for example with regard to the

[1] Cf. the medical conception of the 'body-image' which each of us is supposed to have in this present life. Might we continue to have it after death, if we survive?

kind of spatial properties it may be supposed to have. In the second theory, the analogy we use is a mental or psychological one, the analogy of *dream*-experiences. And here too we have to make any adjustments which seem necessary. Thus we had to bring in telepathy to ensure that the Next World would not be a purely private and subjective one.

But perhaps it does not really make so very much difference which starting-point we choose, the physical one or the psychological one. For I suspect that we are trying to describe something which neither of our two analogies fits perfectly, though both fit it in some degree: we are trying to describe something which is intermediate between the physical and the mental as we ordinarily conceive of them. I am inclined to think that this rather strange idea of a *tertium quid* which is neither altogether material nor altogether mental, or is in a way both at once, is needed in other departments of psychical research as well: for instance when we are considering apparitions, or the phenomena of physical mediumship. It has been said that in the phenomena of materialization 'we see the subjective walking about the room': a strange and suggestive remark (though I confess I wish that these phenomena were better attested).

One may even suspect that if we understood these difficult problems better, we might find ourselves compelled to postulate a *series* of intermediate degrees between the realm of pure thought at the top and the completely material realm at the bottom. Some such postulate is made in the metaphysics of Neoplatonism: and it is worth while to notice that, of all the traditional Western philosophical systems, Neoplatonism is the only one which took explicit account of paranormal phenomena. (As a result, some of its exponents were accused by their critics of being magicians.)

THE MEDIUMISTIC 'PICTURE' OF THE NEXT WORLD

May I illustrate this rather wild suggestion about something which is intermediate between mind and matter? Our empirical evidence for survival—or at least a psychical researcher's evidence for it—comes largely from mediumistic communications, including those which take the form of automatic writing. Now I think mediumistic communications do suggest strongly that there are many Next Worlds, differing with the different desires and memories of their inhabitants. If this were not so, the many different descriptions of the after-life which we get from different ostensible communicators would be quite irreconcilable. But they can easily be made consistent if we suppose that ostensible communicator A is describing the particular Next World which is experienced by him and others like-minded with him, while ostensible communicator B is describing the rather different or very different Next World which *he* experiences—he and those who are like-minded with *him*.

Religious traditions, both Western and Eastern, suggest a similar view. They usually lay stress on the moral aspects of the next life, and insist that after death each person gets the pleasant experiences which are the consequences of his good deeds on earth, and the unpleasant experiences which are the consequences of his misdeeds. It is not easy to see how this could be arranged, unless the after-death world experienced by a particular person is correlated pretty closely with the memories and the moral character of that person. Indeed, we are sometimes told that after death each person 'goes to his own place'. It does look as if there must be *many* Next Worlds, and not just one, if there is a life after death at all.

It follows from this, I think, that the objects we shall be aware of in the next life (if there is one) must be rather different from the ordinary material objects which we are aware of now, even though they may resemble these in having spatial and temporal properties, and secondary qualities such as colour, temperature, and fragrance. So if we insist on thinking of them as *material* objects, we must at any rate admit that this is a kind of matter very different from the matter we are familiar with in our present earthly life. For it seems that this 'Next World' matter has what has been called an *ideoplastic* character. It is responsive, as it were, to the thoughts, memories, and desires of the discarnate persons who perceive it, and the particular form it takes depends on the kind of person that one is. Surely it does look very like 'such stuff as dreams are made on'. In other words, it has at least some of the properties of mental images. Even though we start from what I called the physical analogy, we end with something not very unlike a dream-world. This is what I had in mind when I said earlier that the two theories of the Next World, the quasi-physical theory and the mental-image theory, do indeed have very different starting-points, but if both of them are worked out fully they meet in the middle; and we are left with the conclusion that the Next World is neither quite a physical world nor quite a dream-world, but betwixt and between, with some of the characteristics of both.

A WISH-FULFILMENT WORLD

In conclusion, it is worth while to point out once again that the belief in a life after death is not necessarily a comforting one at all. One might think that it would be, if each person after death experiences the kind of Next World which corresponds to his own desires and emotions. Would not such a world be a wish-fulfilment world, and could anything be more agreeable than that? Alas! it depends what sort of wishes they are. It is quite possible to get what one wishes, and find no satisfaction in it when one gets it. If our desires are cruel and destructive, even if they are merely self-centred without being malevolent, we shall get little satisfaction from their fulfilment. Let us think of dreams again; for even though the Next World, on the view we are discussing, is not quite a dream-world, it is at any rate somewhat like one. According to the Depth-Psychologists the dreams we have now are wish-fulfilments. Nevertheless, they can be exceedingly unpleasant. And what would happen if the barrier between the conscious and the unconscious were removed, as perhaps it will be when there is no longer any need to adjust ourselves to a physical environment, as we have to do in this present life? Desires which are now repressed, at least in our waking hours, would be free to fulfil themselves without hindrance. It is conceivable, I think, that some people's Next World would be very like a nightmare, only worse, because it would be a nightmare from which one could not wake up; and it might well be a very terrifying nightmare indeed. I have deliberately abstained from speculating about Hell in these lectures (we shall do well to leave that subject to the theologians); but, at any rate in the after-life which I have been trying to depict to you, there is plenty of room for a pretty unpleasant Purgatory, or rather for many different ones to suit the many different sorts of evil desires and emotions which there are.

I will end by reminding you of what I said earlier: in the controversy about survival there are wishful thinkers on both sides. It is no wonder that some people dislike the very idea of life after death. We have only to consider how extremely unpleasant some of the many Next Worlds might be.

No doubt there would be room for many different Paradises, as well as many different Purgatories. But it will not do to look only at the bright side of the picture, as if life after death (assuming there is one) were just a happy holiday for us all.

APPENDIX

THE POST-RESURRECTION APPEARANCES

I QUOTE the celebrated passage in 1 Corinthians 15: 3–8. Here St. Paul says that he passed on to his Corinthian converts what he had himself been told: 'that Christ rose [ἐγήγερται—literally, 'woke up'] on the third day, that he was seen of Cephas, then of the Twelve; after that, he was seen of above five hundred brethren at once, of whom the greater part remain unto this present day, but some are fallen asleep; after that, he was seen of James, then of all the apostles. And last of all he was seen of me also, as of one born out of due time.'

We notice that the evidence he quotes is purely visual. Indeed, its visual character is emphasized. The word ὤφθη, 'was seen by' or 'visually appeared to', is used four times. There is no suggestion that the post-Resurrection body of Jesus was tangible too, nor that it was in any sense a material entity, though St. Paul does insist that it was in some degree a *public* entity ('seen of all the apostles', 'seen of above five hundred brethren at once'). He does not even say that it was audible, that the Risen Lord was heard to speak, although in the description of St. Paul's own experience at the Gate of Damascus, in Acts 9, we are told that the Lord did speak to him, and indeed that there was a brief conversation between them.

Perhaps we may put it in this way: in 1 Corinthians 15 nothing is said about any kind of *social* relation between the Risen Lord and the percipients. All the experiences referred to are purely visual. But in the Gospel narratives there is a social relation between the Risen Lord and the percipients. They not only see him, they meet him. He speaks to them. Indeed, in the Emmaus narrative there is a long discussion between the Lord and the two percipients. Questions are asked and they are answered. It might be argued, I think, that seeing without discussion is less evidential than seeing combined with discussion. For the question here was not merely 'Is this a real object, or is it a hallucination?'. The question in the percipients' minds was 'Is this a real person, and moreover a person whom we know and love?'.

The same is true of St. Paul's own experience at the Gate of Damascus as it is described in Acts 9. There is a conversation between St. Paul and the Risen Lord. St. Paul asks two questions: 'Who art thou, Lord?' and 'What wilt thou have me to do?'—and receives replies to both. This too is a social experience, and indeed that is the most important thing about it.

THE POST-RESURRECTION APPEARANCES IN THE GOSPELS

If we now turn to the post-Resurrection appearances described in the Gospels, and compare them with those mentioned by St. Paul in 1 Corinthians 15, we are at first inclined to think that the difference between them is this: St. Paul's evidence in that chapter is purely visual. He uses the word ὤφθη, 'was seen by . . .' or 'visually appeared to . . .', and emphasizes it, for he uses it four times. In the Gospels, on the other hand, it seems to be maintained that the body of the Risen Lord is *tangible*, that he himself said so and even invited the disciples to touch him ('Handle me and see', where 'see' means 'verify it for yourselves'). This tactual evidence would convince them that he himself was really there among them, in their company: not merely 'a spirit' (πνεῦμα), 'for a spirit has not flesh and bones as you see me to have'—but himself, in person. A 'spirit', I take it, is not a Cartesian *res cogitans* (something totally devoid of *spatial* properties). A more adequate translation of πνεῦμα would be the word 'ghost'. A ghost, as popularly conceived, is a spatial entity. It resembles an ordinary human body in its *visible* properties, but it is not tangible.

But despite the words 'Handle me and see', in the Gospels there is only one case in which the body of the Risen Lord *is* actually touched. The women 'clasped his feet and worshipped him' (Matthew 28: 9). Does this suggest, perhaps, that the Lord's post-Resurrection body was only tangible to loving hands? St. Thomas, though he had said that nothing but tactual evidence would convince him, does not seem to have obtained it when the opportunity was given to him. Instead he just said, 'My Lord and my God.' It seems that what he really wanted was perpetual evidence. Hitherto he had only had the evidence of testimony, for he had been absent when the earlier appearances occurred.

In the Gospel narrations of the post-Resurrection appearances there is one other passage about tactual evidence which must be mentioned, the *noli me tangere* passage in John 20: 17: 'Touch me not, for I am not yet ascended to my Father.' I must confess that I am completely puzzled by this. If the Lord said this to Mary Magdalene, why did he say to others 'Handle me and see'? And why did he allow other women to 'clasp his feet and worship him' long before his Ascension?

Of all the post-Resurrection narratives, the one which is most easily credible, at least to a psychical researcher, is the Emmaus narrative in Luke 24: 13–35.[1] That is because the phenomena reported are purely visual and auditory. Nothing at all is said about tangibility. The only puzzling episode is the breaking of the bread. Was the bread physically broken? Or was this too a purely apparitional event? I suspect that it was.

The other Gospel narratives, however, not only emphasize the tangibility of the Lord's post-Resurrection body—they also insist that it has at least some of the causal properties which a normal living human organism would have. That seems to be the point of the passage in Luke 24: 41–2 in which the Risen Lord asks, 'Have you anything to eat?' They give him a piece of broiled (baked?) fish ($\dot{\iota}\chi\theta\acute{\upsilon}os$ $\dot{o}\pi\tauo\hat{\upsilon}$ $\mu\acute{e}\rhoos$) and he eats it before them. In John 21, however—after the miraculous draught of fishes in the Sea of Tiberias— Jesus says to the disciples 'Come and dine', and gives them bread and fish. This 'giving' seems to be a perfectly normal physical action. But apparently on this occasion he did not himself eat. At any rate, it is not said that he did.

THE EMPTY TOMB

But though the Christ's post-Resurrection body does seem to have had some of the properties of a normal physical organism (enough of them, perhaps, to show that a purely apparitional theory will not explain all the phenomena reported), it seems to have had other properties which are very difficult to understand. We must now consider the most puzzling of all the problems about the Resurrection: the empty tomb. What became of the body which died on the Cross? Shall we say that in the tomb it was

[1] There is also a brief reference to it in Mark 16: 12.

'de-materialized' and then 're-materialized' during those two and a half days, and that the re-materialized body was *visibly* similar to the one which had been laid in the tomb but in other ways was very different (for instance, 'alive for ever more')?

But what exactly do we mean by these words 'de-materialized' and 're-materialized'? What becomes of a material object when it is in its de-materialized state? Are we to say that it just ceases to exist altogether for a time, and then a new material object comes into existence, very like the old one in some ways but very unlike it in others?

It is true that recent developments in physics have greatly altered traditional conceptions of matter, but do they throw any light on this problem? What kind of constituents does a 'de-materialized' object have in its de-materialized state? Do they still have *spatial* properties? And what kind of changes occur in them when and if it is later 're-materialized'?

But suppose we do try to think of these very extraordinary events in this way, making use of these puzzling concepts of 'de-materialization' and 're-materialization' (and I do not know what other concepts we might use instead). What conclusions can we then draw about the nature of the Lord's post-Resurrection body? We shall have to say that it was very different from the pre-Resurrection body in its *causal* properties. Yet it was very similar to the pre-Resurrection body in its *perceptible* properties. For the Risen Lord was recognized by his friends, though not always immediately (there is the curious passage in John 26 : 15, where Mary Magdalene at first 'supposes him to be the gardener'). The post-Resurrection body was visible, and apparently tangible also, though there is only one passage in which it is actually touched. 'The women clasped his feet and worshipped him', ἐκράτησαν αὐτοῦ τοὺς πόδας (Matthew 28 : 9).[1] The rendering 'clasped' seems rather too weak; 'grasped' or 'took hold of' might be more accurate.

But what are we to say about its causal properties? Some of them were very similar to those of a normal human body. The Risen Lord could speak and even eat. But his post-Resurrection body also had other causal properties very different from those which a normal human body has. In one passage we are told that it appeared in a room 'the doors being shut' (John 20 : 19); and when the Risen Lord 'went before them into Galilee (Mark 16 : 7),

---

[1] 'held him by the feet', A.V.

how did he go there? We are told that the disciples did find him there some time afterwards.

The narrative in Acts 12, where St. Peter is delivered from prison by an angel, suggests that angels have a somewhat extraordinary property which might be described as 'four-dimensional mobility' (the angel arrives in the prison cell without opening the door). If so, one might argue that *a fortiori* the post-Resurrection body of the Lord would also have four-dimensional mobility.

INDEX

Abelard, P., 5, 84
Achilles, dissatisfied with life after death, 78
Acting 'as if' without believing, 73–4
Actions which are neither right nor wrong, 17
Agnostic's prayer, 72
Anselm, St., 41
Answers to prayer, and coincidences, 45; 'miraculous' theory of, 45–6
Archimedes, 9
'Ask and ye shall receive', 40–1, 65–6
Augustine, St., 67, 76, 95
Automatic speech and writing, 22
Awe, 5

Behaviourism and religion, 67
Biological utility of fear, 2–3
Buddhism and petitionary prayer, 39 n., 54
Burke, E., on the sublime, 6
Butler, J., 10

Camouflage, 2–3
Causal laws, 36
Cave ne eas, 22
Censorship of paranormal impressions, 23–5, 27–8, 34
Coincidences and answers to prayer, 45
Colouring, protective, 2–3
Commands and ignorance, 18
Common unconscious and telepathy, 50–3
Complex ideas, 51
Concept of God, development of, 15–16
'Creative' thinking, 51
Cumulo-nimbus cloud, 6

Da quod jubes, 95
Deity, development of, concept of, 15–17
Delphic priestess, 33–4

Dies irae, 88 n., 96–7
Dieu des philosophes et des savans, 71
Disbelief in life after death, 78–97
Divine commands and morality, 17–20
Dixit insipiens . . ., 41

'Each goes to his own place', 89
Einstein, A., 52
Emergence of paranormal impressions, 22, 25–30
Entertaining of propositions, 38–9
Erith, village of, 61–3, 72, 73
Eternal bliss, 83–5
Eternal Life: quality and duration, 94
Eternal rest, 85
Ethelred the Unready, 10

Faith, 'eye of', 63–4
Fear and love combined, 1–2, 5
Fear and tenderness, 8
Fear, biological utility of, 2–3; cognitive character of, 3
Fear of God, beginning of wisdom, 1–20
Fear of Hell, 82–3
Fear 'on behalf of . . .', 7
Fiat lux, 18
Freud, S., 49

God, development of concept of, 15–17; fear of, beginning of wisdom, ch. 1; 'not far from every one of us', 70; 'of Abraham, Isaac and Jacob', 71; seeking for, 65–70
Gospel, 'good news', 93

Hallucinations, telepathic, 47, 53
Hart and water-brooks, 4
Hell, fear of, 82–3
Hinayana Buddhism, 39 n.
Homer, on post-mortem state of Achilles, 78
Hope and knowledge, 18